BACKCOUNTRY SKI!
WASHINGTON

THE BEST TRAILS & DESCENTS
FOR FREE-HEELERS & SNOWBOARDERS

SEABURY BLAIR, JR.

SASQUATCH BOOKS
SEATTLE

Printed in the United States of America
Distributed in Canada by Raincoast Books, Ltd.
02 01 00 99   5 4 3 2

Cover, interior design, and composition: Kate Basart
Cover photograph: Scott F. Wicklund
Backcover photograph: Josh Eldridge
Interior photographs: Seabury Blair, Jr., Josh Eldridge, Marlene Kocur
Mapmaker: Marlene Kocur

Library of Congress Cataloging in Publication Data

Blair, Seabury,
        Backcountry ski! Washington: the best trails & descents for free-heelers & snowboarders/
        Seabury Blair, Jr.
            p.   cm.
        Includes bibliographical references (p.   )
        ISBN: 1-57061-151-3 (alk. paper)
        1. Cross-country skiing—Washington (State)—Guidebooks. 2. Cross-country ski trails—
        Washington (State)—Guidebooks. 3. Cross-country skiing—Cascade Range—Guidebooks.
        4. Cross-country ski trails—Cascade Range—Guidebooks. 5. Cross-country skiing—Wash-
        ington (State)—Olympic Mountains—Guidebooks. 6. Cross-country ski trails—Washington
        (State)—Olympic Mountains—Guidebooks. 7. Washington (State)—Guidebooks. 8. Cascade
        Range—Guidebooks. 9. Olympic Mountains (Wash.)—Guidebooks. I. Title.
        GV854.5.W33B53 1998
        917.9704'43—dc21   98-28096

IMPORTANT NOTE: Please use common sense. Read the section on Safety and Preparation in the beginning of this book, and sign up for an avalanche course, if you haven't taken one already, *before* you venture out into the backcountry. No guidebook can act as a substitute for experience, careful planning, and appropriate training. There is inherent danger in the backcountry activities described in this book and readers must assume responsibility for their own actions and safety. Changing or unfavorable conditions in weather, road conditions, and—especially—potential for an avalanche cannot be anticipated by the author or publisher, but should be considered by any outdoor participants. The author and publisher will not be responsible for the safety of users of this guide.

SASQUATCH BOOKS
615 Second Avenue
Seattle, WA 98104
(206) 467-4300
www.SasquatchBooks.com
books@SasquatchBooks.com

Sasquatch Books publishes high-quality adult nonfiction and children's books related to the North-west (Alaska to San Francisco). For more information about Sasquatch Books titles, contact us at the address above, or view our site on the World Wide Web.

Contents

"The best way to deal with avalanches," he writes, "is to avoid them completely."

Driving Conditions

While an avalanche is the most dramatic of all the risks you take in the white backcountry, it won't likely be the one to harm you. Fatigue, exposure, or lack of information about your route are much more likely culprits. Remember that most injuries occur in the afternoon, after a day of skiing or riding. Make your last run or glide your last mile in your mind, reclining by the fire with your favorite hot beverage. As we all know, the biggest danger to those who enjoy the winter backcountry face is the drive to and from the trailhead.

And, of course, that drive can be especially daunting when the snow is falling and everyone is rushing to his or her own favorite powder stash. Check the weather forecast, (206) 526-6087, or get the information online at www.gorp.com/wow/.

And check the highway conditions in snow country. They can change rapidly. Call the state Department of Transportation mountain pass report in season, (888) 766-4636, or visit their Web site at www.wsdot.wa.gov/sno-info.

It is one of life's little ironies that the best times for playing in wild snow are often the worst times for driving in it. Fortunately, many of the drivers who ply the roads during these times are experienced at snow travel, both on the road and in the backcountry. They know the meaning of all the traction advisories issued by the Department of Transportation (or National Park Service) and enforced by Washington State troopers (or National Park rangers). The advisories are posted on signs along the roads leading to all the routes in this book:

"Traction devices advised": If you are smart, you'll have tires marked with an "M and S" designation on the power wheels. For maximum traction, you'll also have them on the steering wheels, or rear wheels if you've got front-wheel drive. Or you'll have chains mounted on the power wheels.

If you are not smart, you will not have the above equipment and may legally proceed past the advisory to your destination or the first snowbank you slide into, whichever comes first.

"Traction devices required": This means if you are not equipped with the tires or chains outlined above, you may not proceed.

"Chains required": This advisory means that in order to proceed, you must have chains mounted on the power wheels of your vehicle. A friendly trooper or ranger is almost always on hand to help you interpret this sign.

If you have four-wheel or all-wheel drive, you can proceed past the "chains required" sign without installing chains—but you must carry chains in the vehicle and be prepared to install them at the trooper's or ranger's discretion. I drive a four-wheel-drive truck and in more than 30 years have never been required to put on chains—except, of course, to get myself unstuck.

Glaciers

Parts of several routes in this book descend glaciers. While any travel on a glacier requires special care to avoid crevasses, descending one on a board or skis—which distribute your weight over a larger area—in the middle of winter does not demand the same kind of attention or equipment you will need in the summer.

Most of the glaciers mentioned in the winter routes are small, and crevasses, if any, are hidden and bridged by consolidated snow. Snow on the western side of the Cascades is subject to alternating freeze-thaw cycles that make the likelihood of falling into a crevasse in wintertime extremely remote—far less likely than on Rocky Mountain or Alaskan glaciers, where snow rarely consolidates like Cascade concrete.

Despite the foregoing, avoid any of the glacier routes mentioned here after long periods of warm weather or rain. Ride them only in the middle of winter, after the storms of February have dumped large quantities of snow over the glacial ice. If you have doubts or concerns, choose a route that does not involve glacier travel.

Surely the greatest danger on the glaciers mentioned here would be encountered on the Nisqually, where some huge crevasses remain open in the winter. The glacier has also retreated in recent years, leaving the snout steeper and etched with cracks. Still, snowriders in the midwinter prefer to descend unroped, steering clear of obvious crevasses and avoiding extreme sags and dips in the snow that often indicate an underlying crevasse.

The section on snowriding in spring and summer at the end of this book outlines a number of routes on glaciers. For the most part, these glaciers are "remnant" ice fields that are no longer growing. Their crevasses—if any—are easily avoided.

The exceptions might be the Emmons or Carbon Glaciers—but snowriders should not attempt those massive ice floes without experience. Those who do should be well versed and practiced in crevasse rescue, self-rescue, roped travel, and ice ax management. These are mountaineering skills required on routes that are beyond the scope of this book.

Of greater concern than crevasses are the motes and cracks that open on snowfields between rock and the white stuff. Rock that absorbs and retains heat longer than snow melts wide voids between the snow and rock. While you would avoid these as a matter of course, the danger is that you could fall and slide into one.

Another real danger—one that is responsible for at least two deaths to snowboarders in recent years—is falling into a tree well. Pockets of air form around trees as snow falls on them, and the lower branches sometimes create large hidden caves in the snow at the base of trees that can swallow a skier or boarder.

Typically, snowriders unfortunate enough to fall into a tree well hang upside down from their skis or board. They are unable to reach their bindings to release them. If such an accident were to happen to you, wouldn't you be glad to know your partner is there to help?

My only encounter with a tree well ended happily. I lost one ski and was hanging upside down from the tree, trying to reach the three-pin binding on my other ski. It was an old model with a wire bale, and gravity finally saved me by pulling my foot loose from the binding. I fell into a lump at the base of the tree and was thankful for gravity until that same force pulled the ski out of the tree above and dropped it on my head.

It also made climbing up the tree to the snow surface far more difficult.

Choosing a Route

The alpine slopes suggested here will entertain and challenge intermediates, and some experts, too, on boards, telemark, or randonee gear. The white ways described here should fit your touring skis if you have intermediate skills. I've tried to include opportunities for both downhill and touring experiences on many of the routes, and I have personally tested all of them—even tasted more than I care to admit. Most of these taste tests were conducted using the deep snow facial analysis system I have developed over more than four decades on (or under) Washington's wild snow.

While many of the slopes are several miles from the trailhead, others will allow you to step out of the car and onto your skis or board. All the slopes share one thing: No groomer has touched them. Though perhaps packed by snowmobiles or tracked by other snowriders or gliders, these routes and hills may not appeal to track skiers and skaters.

Ride, glide, or stride these hills and trails and you may find yourself setting the track. But isn't that what backcountry snow play is all about?

The Routes

Here's an explanation of the brief outlines of the routes and runs that appear at the beginning of each description.

Rip Factor ❄

The snowflake icons at the top of the page quickly identify the best slopes. This is an attempt to quantify the overall difficulty—and hence, amount of fun you'll find—on any given slope. Each hill will be rated from 1 to 5 with half "rips" in between—with 5 being a slope that is certain to bring you the kind of pleasure most Baptist churches would declare sinful.

The rip factor is a subjective rating based on the length of the run, slope steepness and vertical drop, and the aspect of the slope as it affects quality of the snow. A south-facing slope of equal length, steepness, and vertical drop, for example, might get a lower rating than a north-facing hill that is likely to retain better snow longer.

Distance

This is the round-trip distance from the parking area to the turnaround point and back. A few routes are one way only and the distance is listed as such. If distances differ between the tour and the downhill, the downhill distance appears first for telemarkers and riders.

Base elevation

The elevation above sea level of the parking area.

Elevation gain or loss

The amount of climbing from the parking area. When "Elevation loss" appears, you'll know you descend from the parking area—and get to climb back to the parking lot.

Trail time

The amount of time spent round-trip skiing on the route, exclusive of yo-yo snowriding on the downhill sections.

Trail type

This describes what lies beneath the snow on the approach route to the hill and the tour, if any. You'll find everything from Forest Service roads to state

1 Alta Vista

❄❄❄

Distance:	0.8 mile
Base elevation:	5,400 feet
Elevation gain:	580 feet
Trail time:	30 minutes
Trail type:	Summer trail
Skill level:	Intermediate
Avalanche potential:	Moderate
Traction advisory:	Skins, waxless
Maps:	Green Trails 270S; USGS Mount Rainier East (7.5' series)

Getting There

From Seattle, drive south on I-5 to exit 127 near Tacoma, which leads to State Route 512 east. Once on SR 512, take the first exit, Steele Street, in order to bypass the heaviest traffic along SR 7 in Spanaway and Parkland. Follow Steele Street and Spanaway Loop Road around Parkland and Spanaway and turn south on SR 7 on the southern outskirts of Spanaway. Follow SR 7 south to Elbe,

Big air off Alta Vista.

Mount Rainier

Backcountry snowriding and touring at Mount Rainier can be summed up in one word: Paradise. Winding to 5,400 feet above sea level, the road to Paradise is the second-highest in the state that is open all winter (Sherman Pass, at 5,575 feet, is highest).

The road leads to what is arguably the best backcountry snowriding in the state, with above-timberline alpine bowls, steep alpine glades, and wide-open glacier routes. And when Mother Nature allows, you'll find a 7-mile, 6,500-vertical-foot run that would test the legs of a grizzly bear.

Paradise is one of the few areas in the Cascades where you can step out of your car and ski or ride down from the parking lot. You can also climb more than a mile above the parking area on the Muir Snowfield for glacier or alpine tele-riding found on only a few snow giants in the world.

On days when you can't see your ski tips through the fog, when it is snowing so hard you risk getting wiped out by an avalanche from your windshield, you can ski up the West Side Road or around Longmire or Cougar Rock without worry.

And on days when the sun shines on a fresh frosting of powder, you can climb up to 10,080-foot Camp Muir and make endless thigh-frying turns back down to Paradise. You'll think you're in Heaven.

Route Maps

The map that accompanies each route is *not* a replacement for a Green Trails or USGS map. The route map shows elevation and mileage points to help you find your way, but should always be used in conjunction with one or more of the maps listed for each route.

Map Legend

℗	Parking Area
——	Road
·—·—·	Ski Route
········	Downhill Run Or Alternate Return Route
➔	Direction Of Travel
↰	Turn Around Point
0.5 ➤	Route Mileage
——	Ski Lift
——	Creek Or River
▲	Shelter
=	Gate

Contour Interval 200 Feet / Scale Varies

Washington Sno-Parks

Cross-country skiers, backcountry snowboarders, and snowmobile riders pay through permits and license fees for the clearing of more than 45 parking areas in snow country for nonmotorized winter recreation as well as a number of Sno-Parks used by snowmobile riders.

Sno-Park permits in 1998 were $20 for an annual pass and $7 per day and are **required** at all of the designated Sno-Park areas. Permits are available at more than 125 retailers, including most outdoor recreation stores; or from the Office of Winter Recreation, Washington State Parks and Recreation Commission, 7150 Cleanwater Lane, PO Box 42662, Olympia, WA 98504-2662; (360) 902-8552.

Oregon and Idaho Sno-Park permits are accepted on cars with Oregon or Idaho license plates.

highways in this listing; the term "backcountry" is used when you must rely on your own route-finding skills to reach a destination.

Skill level

A measure of the minimum skill needed for downhilling or touring on a given route. Skill levels include Novice, Intermediate, Advanced, and Expert. If different skill levels are required for downhilling or touring, the downhill level is given first.

Avalanche potential

Although the avalanche risk will be described using the terms adopted by the Northwest Avalanche Center—low, moderate, considerable (which replaces the old "high" category), and extreme—don't be confused. The terms in this book describe the possibility of an avalanche when the Northwest Avalanche Center describes the danger in its daily report as "considerable" or "extreme." Thus, if the avalanche potential listed in this book is "considerable," it is only "considerable" when the Northwest Avalanche Center forecasts a "considerable" or "extreme" danger for that day. The potential here is based on steepness of the slope, its aspect, the ground cover under the snow, and the observed or known avalanche history—not on snow conditions. If you find boilerplate on a slope that is rated as having a "high" avalanche potential, consider the author as having done far too many face-plants.

Traction advisory

This is an attempt to suggest what kinds of skis or traction devices will be helpful in ascending the slopes outlined here. If the route includes both downhill and touring possibilities, the climbing aids for downhill are given first.

Almost all of the routes in this book were originally explored by the author aboard steel-edged Karhu XCD Kinetic waxless skis—but skins would have made any of the hills much easier to climb. Steel edges are a requirement for all the hills. Boarders will find climbing skins essential if using a split board; an acquaintance who guides in British Columbia climbs up the hill on sawed-off randonee skis with indoor-outdoor carpet glued to the bottoms, then packs them up and rides his board down.

Map

The Green Trails maps are listed here, largely because they contain some information about winter routes. U.S. Geological Survey maps may show slopes in greater detail; Custom Correct maps of the Olympic Mountains may also be used there.

then follow SR 706 through Ashford to the Nisqually entrance to Mount Rainier National Park. Be prepared to pay a $10 per carload entrance fee to the park. From the park entrance, follow SR 706 past Longmire to Paradise. This is a two-lane, winding road that climbs 15 miles and 3,000 feet from the park entrance. Carry chains, even if you have four-wheel drive; though park road crews do an excellent job of keeping the route open, chains may sometimes be required at Longmire, Cougar Rock, or the Nisqually bridge.

During winter, the road is closed to uphill traffic at dusk and closed and locked each night. Snowplows clear the road each morning and crews attempt to open it daily by 10 A.M. It may open sooner or later than that, depending upon conditions at Paradise—and during the biggest storms or highest avalanche danger, it may not open at all. If there is the slightest doubt about weather conditions at Paradise, call (360) 569-2211 (and be prepared to play with the voice mail system).

Once at Paradise, drive 200 yards east of the Henry M. Jackson Visitor Center to the large parking lot. Rest rooms, a ranger station, and the Rainier Mountaineering, Inc., guide hut (closed in winter) are located here. Overnight parking is permitted in a section of the lot; ask a ranger.

Allow about three and a half hours from Seattle to Paradise. It will take longer if the gate is late in opening or you have to put on chains.

The Route

0.0 Paradise parking lot

0.4 Alta Vista summit (distance varies according to number of switchbacks)

This hill has been the training ground for backcountry skiers for more than half a century. During World War II, Alta Vista was one of the major slopes used to train members of the 10th Mountain Division.

You can't argue with history. This is a splendid hill even when you can't see where you are going and must navigate back to the parking lot from the sound of inner-tubers' screams or snowplows at work. And it's a splendid hill when you *can* see, and you have only a half day for your snowriding adventure.

From the parking lot, climb northerly to a flat saddle in the ridge just east of Alta Vista, at 5,760 feet. Once at the saddle, switchback up to the summit from the east side.

Alta Vista is a micro-demonstration of all that makes the Paradise area a great place for snowriding. It offers a wide variety of slope aspects. You can plunge off the summit in almost any direction but north and get a great ride.

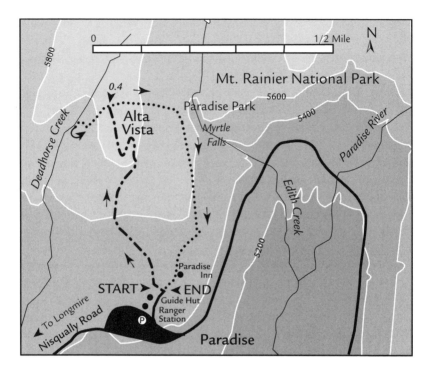

To the west, you'll find an open slope that drops steeply to the Panorama Point Trail. This is a good springtime slope and is best in winter when the snow falls without the usual southwesterly gales.

If you try the easterly side, you'll turn down into Paradise Park. The farther north along the ridge of Alta Vista you go, the steeper and longer the run. The northernmost part of this ridge carries the greatest potential for avalanche.

Boarders appear to enjoy dropping off Alta Vista to the south, along the treed ridge to the saddle. This gives them numerous opportunities to grab major air—"mental-hospital air," as we say in telemark circles—from tree drifts and cornices.

Intermediate telemarkers need only climb to the flat saddle if they wish, then ski off the rounded ridge to the northeast. When visibility is poor, aim for the island of large firs at the bottom of the slope, just to the right of the Edith Creek canyon.

For another good hill from the saddle, ski east along the ridge. This broad crest becomes increasingly steep and drops to the Paradise Inn below, which is closed in winter.

2 MOUNT RAINIER
Panorama Point Loop
❄❄❄

Distance:	2.6 miles
Base elevation:	5,400 feet
Elevation gain:	800 feet
Trail time:	2 hours
Trail type:	Summer trail, backcountry
Skill level:	Intermediate
Avalanche potential:	Moderate
Traction advisory:	Skins, waxless
Maps:	Green Trails 270S; USGS Mount Rainier East (7.5' series)

Getting There

From Seattle, drive south on I-5 to exit 127 near Tacoma, which leads to State Route 512 east. Once on SR 512, take the first exit, Steele Street, in order to

The flat saddle in the foreground, center, is the Edith Basin Saddle.

bypass the heaviest traffic along SR 7 in Spanaway and Parkland. Follow Steele Street and Spanaway Loop Road around Parkland and Spanaway and turn south on SR 7 on the southern outskirts of Spanaway. Follow SR 7 south to Elbe, then follow SR 706 through Ashford to the Nisqually entrance to Mount Rainier National Park. Be prepared to pay a $10 per carload entrance fee to the park.

For information about snow and driving conditions inside the park, see the Getting There section for Route 1, Alta Vista.

Once at Paradise, drive 200 yards east of the Henry M. Jackson Visitor Center to the large parking lot. Rest rooms, a ranger station, and the Rainier Mountaineering, Inc., guide hut (closed in winter) are located here. Overnight parking is permitted in a section of the lot; ask a ranger.

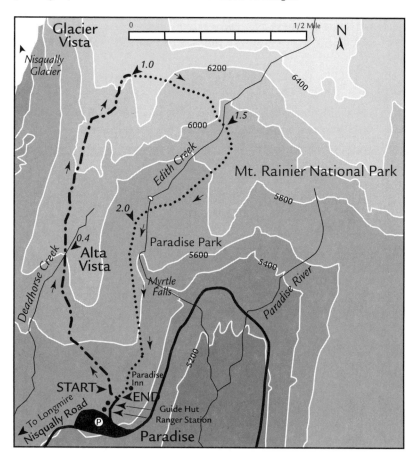

Allow about three and a half hours from Seattle to Paradise. It will take longer if the gate is late in opening or you have to put on chains.

The Route

0.0 Paradise parking lot
0.4 Deadhorse Creek
1.0 Edith Basin saddle
1.5 Edith Creek
2.0 Paradise Park
2.6 Parking lot

The route that loops beneath Alta Vista and Panorama Point makes an excellent introduction to what is arguably the best of Washington's wild snow. When you can see, Rainier hunkers above like an icy giant troll, the Tatoosh Range scratches clouds to the south, and Mounts Adams and St. Helens poke holes in them.

For the first mile, you'll follow what in the summer is the paved trail to Glacier Vista and the beginning of the trail to Camp Muir. In the winter, this trail is buried by as much as 20 feet of snow—but it's marked by orange poles, and ski or snowshoe tracks often make route-finding easy.

On days when you're making the first tracks, however, you'll want to climb to the right of the inner-tube chutes at Paradise in a northwesterly direction to the base of Alta Vista. The broad ridge at the top of the inner-tube chutes can also be followed to the base of Alta Vista.

Traverse under the west slope of Alta Vista at about 5,760 feet and across a sidehill into the broad gully of Deadhorse Creek, at 0.4 mile. Climb up the gully, which is gentle enough that most waxless ski bases will not slip.

Continue climbing, crossing to the left, or west side, of the gully at about 5,800 feet. A drift cornice sometimes forms along the eastern edge of the slope, above the Deadhorse gully.

Climb to a broad saddle at about 6,200 feet and 1.0 mile from the parking area, just below a steep ridge that climbs to Panorama Point. (This ridge is marked by several small trees clinging to the steep hillside about halfway up the slope and is the safest route up Pan. The summer trail to Muir veers to the left at this point to climb under Pan Point to a spot overlooking the Nisqually Glacier before switching back up Pan.)

If you've been climbing with skins, now is the time to stow them away. It's all downhill from here.

Ride into the wide bowl carved by the infant Edith Creek. For a steep shot, traverse from the saddle to the left, or northeast. Avoid this slope in times of high avalanche danger.

For a more gentle descent, turn easterly into the base of the bowl. Avoid traversing too far back to the south; a cornice overlooks Edith Creek here and is frequently used for training Rainier Mountaineering clients in the spring.

The Edith Basin is a good spot for learning the intricacies of the telemark turn and getting a taste of Rainier snow—figuratively speaking, of course. Those seeking more exercise can skin back up and do this hill until their legs wobble.

At the bottom of the basin, ski a gentle grade southeasterly, keeping an island of trees to your right (although a short, steep pitch can be found just to the south of this island). Just past the island, turn south and follow Edith Creek down into a wide, flat basin called Paradise Park. The northeast face of Alta Vista now confronts you. Ski toward the bottom of the basin, aiming toward the spot where Edith Creek turns east and plunges into a rocky canyon and frozen Myrtle Falls to the Paradise River. There's a bridge here in the summer; in winter, simply cross where it's convenient.

Just across the creek, at 2.0 miles and 5,600 feet, you'll find an island of trees guarding the steeper slopes down to the Paradise River. Just to the right, or west, of these trees, is the summer trail leading back to the parking lot.

For more downhill action, ski or ride the round ridge east of the trees down to the road that leads from Paradise around Paradise Valley. Keep right of the cliffs and Myrtle Falls and watch for cliffs just above the road. You'll need to ski up the road.

Those who stay on the trail will find a gentle traverse down to the parking lot. For a more thrilling finish, climb to the top of Alta Vista and ride back to the lot.

3 MOUNT RAINIER
Corkscrew/Nisqually View
❄❄½

Distance:	2.0 miles
Base elevation:	5,400 feet
Elevation gain:	400 feet
Trail time:	1.5 hours
Trail type:	Summer trail, backcountry
Skill level:	Intermediate
Avalanche potential:	Low
Traction advisory:	Skins, waxless, waxable
Maps:	Green Trails 270S; USGS Mount Rainier East (7.5' series)

Getting There

From Seattle, drive south on I-5 to exit 127 near Tacoma, which leads to State Route 512 east. Once on SR 512, take the first exit, Steele Street, in order to bypass the heaviest traffic along SR 7 in Spanaway and Parkland. Follow Steele Street and Spanaway Loop Road around Parkland and Spanaway and turn south on SR 7 on the southern outskirts of Spanaway. Follow SR 7 south to Elbe, then follow SR 706 through Ashford to the Nisqually entrance to Mount Rainier National Park. Be prepared to pay a $10 per carload entrance fee to the park.

For information about snow and driving conditions inside the park, see the Getting There section for Route 1, Alta Vista.

Once at Paradise, drive 200 yards east of the Henry M. Jackson Visitor Center to the large parking lot. Rest rooms, a ranger station, and the Rainier Mountaineering, Inc., guide hut (closed in winter) are located here. Overnight parking is permitted in a section of the lot; ask a ranger.

Allow about three and a half hours from Seattle to Paradise. It will take longer if the gate is late in opening or you have to put on chains.

The Route

0.0 Paradise parking lot
0.4 Deadhorse Creek

0.6 Corkscrew Ridge
1.0 Nisqually view

This southwesterly-facing slope hoards light snow because it is sheltered by trees that both shade the hill and gentle the wind. When soft, light snow can't be found anywhere else on Mount Rainier, you will likely find it here.

Climb beneath Alta Vista on the Panorama Point Trail, to the right of the inner-tube chutes. Follow the trail to a point where Deadhorse Creek gully is just below the trail, about 0.4 mile and 5,700 feet.

Ski or ride down into the creek and climb up the other side to the west-northwest. You'll gain a flat ridge, called Corkscrew Ridge, that trends to the south here. It appears to end in a clump of trees on a flat mound of snow, at about 5,560 feet.

Ski around the trees to find a snow-covered meadow. Divided by a creek gully, this south-facing meadow doglegs to the west about halfway down. It is not known whether this twisting gave the ridge its name or whether it's the way your body will feel after several runs.

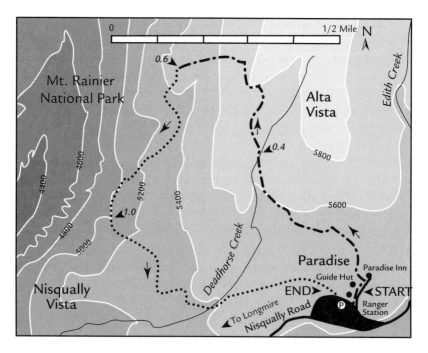

The hill ends at about 5,200 feet, where skiers and boarders can slalom through tightly spaced trees another 200 vertical feet to the edge of a cliff that overlooks the Nisqually Glacier. Here you can either climb back up for another run or traverse south through meadows and trees to pick up the Nisqually Vista Trail, marked by orange poles. This trail leads past summer employee quarters and a snow-measuring station to the Henry M. Jackson Visitor Center.

MOUNT RAINIER
4 Mazama Ridge
❄❄❄

Distance:	3.0 miles
Base elevation:	5,400 feet
Elevation gain:	520 feet
Trail time:	2.5 hours
Trail type:	Park road, trail, backcountry
Skill level:	Intermediate
Avalanche potential:	Considerable
Traction advisory:	Skins, waxless
Maps:	Green Trails 270S; USGS Mount Rainier East (7.5' series)

Mazama Ridge and the Tatoosh Range in the background.

Getting There

From Seattle, drive south on I-5 to exit 127 near Tacoma, which leads to State Route 512 east. Once on SR 512, take the first exit, Steele Street, in order to bypass the heaviest traffic along SR 7 in Spanaway and Parkland. Follow Steele Street and Spanaway Loop Road around Parkland and Spanaway and turn south on SR 7 on the southern outskirts of Spanaway. Follow SR 7 south to Elbe, then follow SR 706 through Ashford to the Nisqually entrance to Mount Rainier National Park. Be prepared to pay a $10 per carload entrance fee to the park.

For information about snow and driving conditions inside the park, see the Getting There section for Route 1, Alta Vista.

Once at Paradise, drive 200 yards east of the Henry M. Jackson Visitor Center to the large parking lot. Rest rooms, a ranger station, and the Rainier Mountaineering, Inc., guide hut (closed in winter) are located here. Overnight parking is permitted in a section of the lot; ask a ranger.

Allow about three and a half hours from Seattle to Paradise. It will take longer if the gate is late in opening or you have to put on chains.

The Route

0.0	Paradise parking lot
0.5	Edith Creek bridge
0.7	First Paradise River bridge
1.1	Base of Mazama
1.5	Mazama Ridge

This is some of the best snowriding within easy reach of the Paradise parking area. Take your skins and spend a day along this ridge. You won't be able to track up half of it unless you're part Pisten-Bulley. (A Pisten-Bulley is a snow-grooming machine—a powerful snow-grooming machine.)

Climb out of the parking lot onto the Paradise Road, under at least 20 feet of snow, at the southeast end. Follow the road around the Paradise Inn on the left to the edge of the hill overlooking the Paradise River valley.

The road drops gently to the north, into the valley. Rounding the first corner to the north, just past the lodge, can be a windblown, blinding experience under certain conditions. This is usually temporary; stay on the road until the ridge shelters you from above, about 100 yards.

Follow the road down into the valley, crossing the Edith Creek bridge at about 0.5 mile to the first Paradise River bridge at about 0.7 mile. Two routes are possible from here.

If downhill thrills are the main goal, cross both Paradise bridges and climb the open avalanche slopes in front of you. These are the slopes you will be riding or skiing, and in times of considerable avalanche danger, they should be avoided.

A second route is to switchback before crossing the second Paradise bridge and climb the broad Paradise Valley, keeping well away from the steep-walled ridge that climbs to the Edith Creek basin on the left. Climb from the bridge at about 5,240 feet into the basin below Sluiskin Falls, at about 5,520 feet and 1.1 miles.

A summer trail and bridge crosses the Paradise River at this point, but snow covers the water most of the winter. Switchback up Mazama Ridge to the east, gaining the crest at about 5,800 feet.

The ridge is gentle and wide along the crest and is a popular camping spot for winter overnighters. Beginning telemarkers will find inviting alpine prac-

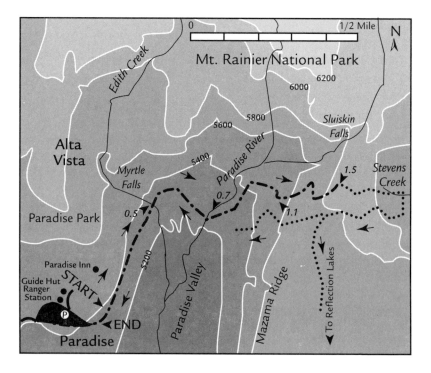

tice slopes, while those looking for more challenging downhill can pick slopes leading back down to Paradise Valley.

Another steeper option is to ride off the ridge to the east, dropping into the bowl formed by the beginnings of Stevens Creek. Avoid this 600-foot vertical slope if avalanche danger is considerable; a "creep" fissure sometimes opens along the crest of the ridge, and snow below may occasionally move faster than a creep.

To reach the open slopes above the Paradise Road, drop about 200 feet back into the Paradise side of the ridge and traverse in meadows to the south at about 5,600 feet, crossing two steep gullies and through trees to the avalanche slopes above the road.

5 MOUNT RAINIER
Reflection Lakes
❄

Distance: 6.8 miles
Base elevation: 5,400 feet
Elevation loss: 600 feet
Trail time: 4 hours
Trail type: Road
Skill level: Novice
Avalanche potential: Moderate
Traction advisory: Waxless
Maps: Green Trails 270S; USGS Mount Rainier East (7.5' series)

Lunch break, Reflection Lakes.

Getting There

From Seattle, drive south on I-5 to exit 127 near Tacoma, which leads to State Route 512 east. Once on SR 512, take the first exit, Steele Street, in order to bypass the heaviest traffic along SR 7 in Spanaway and Parkland. Follow Steele Street and Spanaway Loop Road around Parkland and Spanaway and turn south on SR 7 on the southern outskirts of Spanaway. Follow SR 7 south to Elbe, then follow SR 706 through Ashford to the Nisqually entrance to Mount Rainier National Park. Be prepared to pay a $10 per carload entrance fee to the park.

For information about snow and driving conditions inside the park, see the Getting There section for Route 1, Alta Vista.

Once at Paradise, drive 200 yards east of the Henry M. Jackson Visitor Center to the large parking lot. Rest rooms, a ranger station, and the Rainier Mountaineering, Inc., guide hut (closed in winter) are located here. Overnight parking is permitted in a section of the lot; ask a ranger.

Allow about three and a half hours from Seattle to Paradise. It will take longer if the gate is late in opening or you have to put on chains.

The Route

0.0 Paradise parking lot
0.7 First Paradise River bridge
2.3 Road branches (keep left)
2.5 Inspiration Point
3.4 First Reflection Lake

There are two routes on this pleasant day tour that offers many downhill possibilities for those who take their touring vertically. The first (longer) route is given here. The second, from Narada Falls, cuts off the first 2.5 miles and provides the closest access for the Castle Saddle (Route 13).

The longer route makes the more scenic tour, with sunset views of Rainier—also known as Tahoma by local Native Americans—on the way home. Reflection Lakes is a great turnaround spot, with hills to the north, south, and east for riding or telemarking. Families with young children may choose to stop in Paradise Valley or above Narada Falls for shorter outings.

Ski or snowshoe on the road past the Paradise Inn and turn down to the north into Paradise Valley. Wind sometimes whips clouds into a daunting frenzy as the road turns north above the valley; this is usually a temporary discomfort and is passed in less than 100 yards.

The road descends gently into Paradise Valley, making a good area to test your glide wax against that of your companions. This part of the road is the steepest grade you'll encounter, and you will notice an interesting phenomenon on your return: The road will be twice as steep.

Make a broad turn to the south at the bottom of the valley underneath Mazama Ridge, after crossing the second Paradise River bridge. The road contours above the valley for about a mile before the valley narrows and steepens. Ski around two switchbacks to a road junction at about 2.3 miles.

Turn left here. (The road to the right curves gently down and in about a quarter mile joins the main road to Paradise just above Narada Falls. Going this way makes a good one-way trip if you have two cars or someone to pick you up on the main road.)

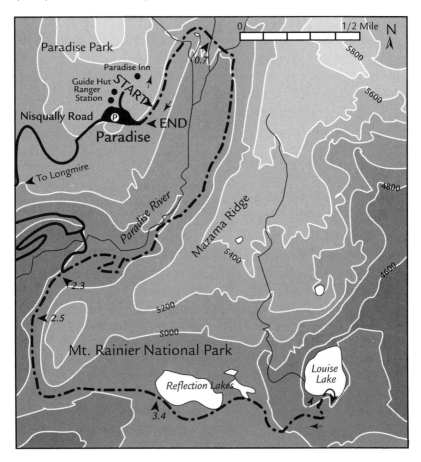

The left branch traverses a steep section above Narada Falls that may cause beginners to wonder if they should have brought crampons. Worry not—the steepest part is less than 50 yards long and leads to a wide, flat area that in the summer is the Inspiration Point parking area. Look to the northwest here to discover how the area got its name.

About a half mile past Inspiration Point, the road rounds the end of Mazama Ridge and turns east to Reflection Lakes. There are five altogether, but the first is the largest and may be the only one discernible in midwinter snow. At 4,854 feet above sea level, the lakes can be crossed on skis most of the winter.

The lakes are a good spot for lunch. Try the south shore on clear days to admire Rainier, the north side for winter sunshine. If you can't make up your mind, plunk down in the middle of the lake and rotate 180 degrees when the mood strikes.

Snowriders looking for steep thrills will find them in the bowl just east of Reflection Lakes, a 280-vertical-foot wall around Louise Lake. This hill is prone to avalanche, and riders should be aware of the current danger before descending. Easiest way back to Reflection Lakes is to cross Louise Lake to the southeast and climb about 120 feet to the Reflection Lakes Road, which passes Louise Lake on the south and descends into Stevens Canyon.

Downhillers can also ascend the north side of Mazama Ridge by climbing north of Reflection Lakes, or climb to the south to the Castle Saddle.

MOUNT RAINIER

6 Paradise Glacier
❄❄❄❄

Distance: 7.2 miles
Base elevation: 5,400 feet
Elevation gain: 2,050 feet
Trail time: 4.5 hours
Trail type: Road, trail, backcountry
Skill level: Intermediate to expert
Avalanche potential: Moderate
Traction advisory: Skins, waxless
Maps: Green Trails 270S; USGS Mount Rainier East (7.5' series)

The route to Cowlitz Rocks passes under Golden Gate, in the foreground.

Getting There

From Seattle, drive south on I-5 to exit 127 near Tacoma, which leads to State Route 512 east. Once on SR 512, take the first exit, Steele Street, in order to bypass the heaviest traffic along SR 7 in Spanaway and Parkland. Follow Steele Street and Spanaway Loop Road around Parkland and Spanaway and turn south on SR 7 on the southern outskirts of Spanaway. Follow SR 7 south to Elbe, then follow SR 706 through Ashford to the Nisqually entrance to Mount Rainier National Park. Be prepared to pay a $10 per carload entrance fee to the park.

For information about snow and driving conditions inside the park, see the Getting There section for Route 1, Alta Vista.

Once at Paradise, drive 200 yards east of the Henry M. Jackson Visitor Center to the large parking lot. Rest rooms, a ranger station, and the Rainier Mountaineering, Inc., guide hut (closed in winter) are located here. Overnight parking is permitted in a section of the lot; ask a ranger.

Allow about three and a half hours from Seattle to Paradise. It will take longer if the gate is late in opening or you have to put on chains.

The Route

0.0 Paradise parking lot
0.7 First Paradise River bridge
1.2 Base of Mazama Ridge
1.6 Sluiskin Falls
2.6 Paradise Glacier Ice Caves site
3.6 Cowlitz Rocks

Here is Rainier skiing at its backcountry best. Boarders on snowshoes, however, may think this a long trek. Some riders may also find the almost mile-long contour from the Paradise Glacier to Sluiskin Falls too flat on the descent.

Also, it is wise not to attempt this route when visibility is poor, especially if you can't navigate by compass or GPS. Once beyond Sluiskin Falls, you are above timberline. Snow, fog, or whiteout can make route-finding a challenge. There are so many other hills at Rainier; this one is best saved for a clear, sunny day.

Begin by skiing or riding down the road to the first Paradise River bridge and climbing north to the base of Mazama Ridge. Climb the ridge to the summit at about 5,800 feet. (For a more detailed description of this part of the route, see Route 4, Mazama Ridge.)

Once on the ridge crest, turn north, staying on the crest as it narrows above the southeast-facing Stevens Creek bowl and the Paradise River as it arcs over Sluiskin Falls, named for a Native American involved in early Rainier exploration. Follow this broad basin, once covered by the retreating Paradise

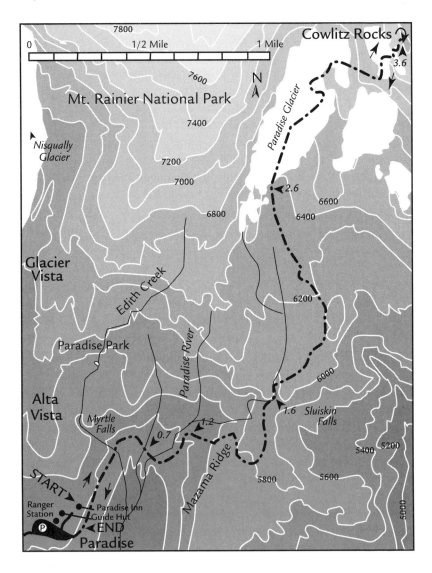

Glacier, to the north for almost another mile to the base of the glacier, about 6,400 feet.

Here is the site of the old Paradise Ice Caves, now closed and partially—if not completely—collapsed.

Climb the snow-covered, crevasse-free glacier, trending gradually to the northeast and, at about 7,000 feet, begin switching back and climbing to the summit of 7,450-foot Cowlitz Rocks. This high point in the ridge cleaves the Paradise and Cowlitz Glaciers and provides stunning views to the north across the Cowlitz to Whitman Crest, Panhandle Gap, and up the Cowlitz to Camp Muir and Mount Rainier.

Sit. Have lunch. Golly, Beaver, get ready for a swell ride home.

7 MOUNT RAINIER
Paradise Valley
❄ ❄ ❄

Distance:	0.4 mile
Base elevation:	5,400 feet
Elevation loss:	360 feet
Trail time:	45 minutes
Trail type:	Backcountry
Skill level:	Advanced
Avalanche potential:	Considerable
Traction advisory:	Skins, waxless
Maps:	Green Trails 270S; USGS Mount Rainier East (7.5' series)

Getting There

From Seattle, drive south on I-5 to exit 127 near Tacoma, which leads to State Route 512 east. Once on SR 512, take the first exit, Steele Street, in order to bypass the heaviest traffic along SR 7 in Spanaway and Parkland. Follow

Paradise, on the right, and Mazama Ridge, left, surround Paradise Valley.

Steele Street and Spanaway Loop Road around Parkland and Spanaway and turn south on SR 7 on the southern outskirts of Spanaway. Follow SR 7 south to Elbe, then follow SR 706 through Ashford to the Nisqually entrance to Mount Rainier National Park. Be prepared to pay a $10 per carload entrance fee to the park.

For information about snow and driving conditions inside the park, see the Getting There section for Route 1, Alta Vista.

Once at Paradise, drive 200 yards east of the Henry M. Jackson Visitor Center to the large parking lot. Rest rooms, a ranger station, and the Rainier Mountaineering, Inc., guide hut (closed in winter) are located here. Overnight parking is permitted in a section of the lot; ask a ranger.

Allow about three and a half hours from Seattle to Paradise. It will take longer if the gate is late in opening or you have to put on chains.

The Route

0.0 Paradise parking lot
0.2 Paradise Valley

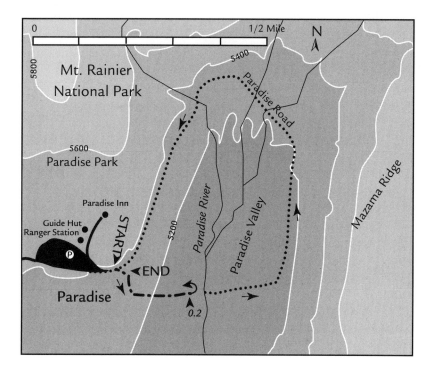

Here's one for snowriders who like to get up late and for anyone who arrives at Paradise to find Mother Nature is allowing route-finding only by using the Braille method. The steep slope down to the Paradise River, east of the parking lot, can provide a whole weekend's worth of yo-yo snowriding without crossing your track.

Start by skiing or snowshoeing east from the parking lot to the spot where the road turns north into Paradise Valley. While any part of the hill that now confronts you may be descended, you'll find a turn south along the ridge crest will treat you to a hillside sheltered from the prevailing winds by trees.

Boarders will want to switchback up the hill for another ride. Skiers may wish to kick and glide across the flat Paradise Valley floor to the east, find a snow bridge across the creek, and ascend the base of Mazama Ridge to the Paradise Road. You can tour up the road for another descent.

Still another way of gaining the Paradise Road from the valley is to ski north up the valley floor, along the Paradise River, gaining the road as it curves around to cross the creek.

MOUNT RAINIER
8 | Golden Gate Bowls
❄❄❄❄

Distance:	2.8 miles
Base elevation:	5,400 feet
Elevation gain:	1,000 feet
Trail time:	3 hours
Trail type:	Summer trail, backcountry
Skill level:	Advanced
Avalanche potential:	Considerable
Traction advisory:	Skins, waxless
Maps:	Green Trails 270S; USGS Mount Rainier East (7.5' series)

Golden Gate bowl climbs to the ridge at right, center.

Getting There

From Seattle, drive south on I-5 to exit 127 near Tacoma, which leads to State Route 512 east. Once on SR 512, take the first exit, Steele Street, in order to bypass the heaviest traffic along SR 7 in Spanaway and Parkland. Follow Steele Street and Spanaway Loop Road around Parkland and Spanaway and turn south on SR 7 on the southern outskirts of Spanaway. Follow SR 7 south to Elbe, then follow SR 706 through Ashford to the Nisqually entrance to Mount Rainier National Park. Be prepared to pay a $10 per carload entrance fee to the park.

For information about snow and driving conditions inside the park, see the Getting There section for Route 1, Alta Vista.

Once at Paradise, drive 200 yards east of the Henry M. Jackson Visitor Center to the large parking lot. Rest rooms, a ranger station, and the Rainier Mountaineering, Inc., guide hut (closed in winter) are located here. Overnight parking is permitted in a section of the lot; ask a ranger.

Allow about three and a half hours from Seattle to Paradise. It will take longer if the gate is late in opening or you have to put on chains.

The Route

0.0   Paradise parking lot
0.4   Paradise Park
0.9   Edith Creek basin
1.4   Golden Gate

Two steep, 400-vertical-foot bowls wait for snowriders to leave their tracks so the setting winter sun can make them visible all the way to Alta Vista.

Follow the summer trail around the east ridge of Alta Vista, past Paradise Inn. Just past the lodge, the trail turns north and climbs gently into Paradise Park. If you're setting the track, aim toward a knoll with an island of trees at the east edge. This group of trees is a landmark when returning from Edith Creek basin or skiing off Alta Vista to the east.

Past the trees is Edith Creek, tumbling in a frozen rush over Myrtle Falls. Cross the creek above the falls and climb into the broad bowl to the north. Aim for the lowest point, marked on the west by a knoll and another tree island at about 5,900 feet. The first Golden Gate bowl is directly ahead.

At about 6,000 feet, you can begin switching back up the face of the bowl. A steep gully and ridge on the east side of the bowl leads toward the summit to the spot where, at about 6,400 feet, the summer trail to Golden Gate joins the Skyline Trail. The top of this section is frequently sculpted by the wind into four-foot drifts.

The surface of this south-facing bowl sweeps all the way west to a steep ridge leading to Panorama Point. A wide gully in the middle of the bowl marks the birthplace of Edith Creek and may make an interesting run for riders.

Because the bowl is exposed to prevailing winds, the best winter snow is often found in the steep gully along the east ridge of the bowl. Stay just west of the tree line along the ridge and flirt with gravity.

To reach the second bowl, cross the tree line to the east. You'll find that in midwinter, the trees capture the driven snow and deposit it along the west side of the bowl. In the spring, both bowls are among the first to provide excellent corn snow.

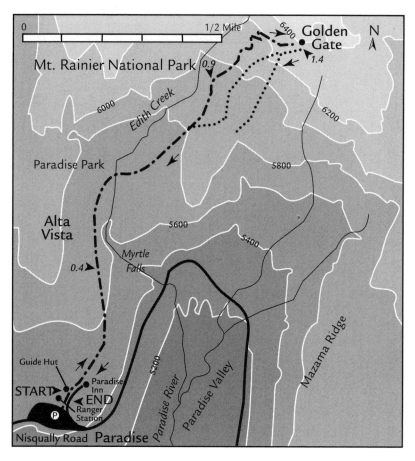

MOUNT RAINIER
9 | Edith's Rib
❄❄❄❄

Distance:	2.2 miles
Base elevation:	5,400 feet
Elevation gain:	600 feet
Trail time:	1.5 hours
Trail type:	Summer trail, backcountry
Skill level:	Advanced
Avalanche potential:	Moderate
Traction advisory:	Skins, waxless
Maps:	Green Trails 270S; USGS Mount Rainier East (7.5' series)

The route to Edith's Rib crosses the flats below Golden Gate.

Getting There

From Seattle, drive south on I-5 to exit 127 near Tacoma, which leads to State Route 512 east. Once on SR 512, take the first exit, Steele Street, in order to bypass the heaviest traffic along SR 7 in Spanaway and Parkland. Follow Steele Street and Spanaway Loop Road around Parkland and Spanaway and turn south on SR 7 on the southern outskirts of Spanaway. Follow SR 7 south to Elbe, then follow SR 706 through Ashford to the Nisqually entrance to Mount Rainier National Park. Be prepared to pay a $10 per carload entrance fee to the park.

For information about snow and driving conditions inside the park, see the Getting There section for Route 1, Alta Vista.

Once at Paradise, drive 200 yards east of the Henry M. Jackson Visitor Center to the large parking lot. Rest rooms, a ranger station, and the Rainier Mountaineering, Inc., guide hut (closed in winter) are located here. Overnight parking is permitted in a section of the lot; ask a ranger.

Allow about three and a half hours from Seattle to Paradise. It will take longer if the gate is late in opening or you have to put on chains.

The Route

0.0 Paradise parking lot
0.4 Paradise Park
0.9 Edith Creek basin
1.1 Edith's Rib

This run, from a ridge that divides the Edith Creek basin and one of the Paradise River tributaries, was one of Paradise ranger Bundy Phillips's favorites before he moved south. It offers several aspects, and boarders will find a couple of massive half-pipes carved into the snow by Mother Nature.

Follow the directions given in the description for Golden Gate Bowls (Route 8) and climb into the Edith Creek basin, a broad bowl under Golden Gate and Panorama Point at about 6,000 feet.

As the face of the bowl steepens, turn east and contour at about 6,000 feet around the steep ridge dropping from Golden Gate into a second bowl. Look east to the eastern shoulder of the second bowl to see an island of trees on the ridgeline at 6,000 feet. These trees mark the start of your downhill run from Edith's Rib.

Several descents are possible from this knoll. You can swoop due south, dropping all the way to the Paradise Road, 800 feet below. You can contour around the knoll to the north, then turn downhill to the east, dropping into the upper Paradise River valley at the base of Mazama Ridge. The biggest gully for half-pipe thrills begins just north of this run and drops steeply to the east.

Skiers with skins looking for another ride can climb back to the knoll and return through Edith Basin and Paradise Park. Those in a touring mode can drop to the Paradise Road and kick and glide up it to the parking lot. It's about seven-tenths of a mile to the lot from the second bridge across Paradise River.

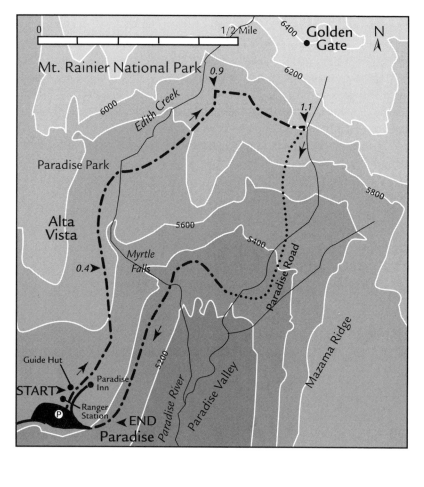

10 MOUNT RAINIER
Devil's Dip
❅❅❅

Distance:	2.0 miles
Base elevation:	5,400 feet
Elevation loss:	800 feet
Trail time:	1.5 hours
Trail type:	Summer trail
Skill level:	Intermediate
Avalanche potential:	Moderate
Traction advisory:	Skins, waxless
Maps:	Green Trails 270S; USGS Mount Rainier East (7.5' series)

Getting There

From Seattle, drive south on I-5 to exit 127 near Tacoma, which leads to State Route 512 east. Once on SR 512, take the first exit, Steele Street, in order to bypass the heaviest traffic along SR 7 in Spanaway and Parkland. Follow Steele Street and Spanaway Loop Road around Parkland and Spanaway and turn south on SR 7 on the southern outskirts of Spanaway. Follow SR 7 south to Elbe, then follow SR 706 through Ashford to the Nisqually entrance to Mount Rainier National Park. Be prepared to pay a $10 per carload entrance fee to the park.

For information about snow and driving conditions inside the park, see the Getting There section for Route 1, Alta Vista.

Once at Paradise, drive 200 yards east of the Henry M. Jackson Visitor Center to the large parking lot. Rest rooms, a ranger station, and the Rainier Mountaineering, Inc., guide hut (closed in winter) are located here. Overnight parking is permitted in a section of the lot; ask a ranger.

Allow about three and a half hours from Seattle to Paradise. It will take longer if the gate is late in opening or you have to put on chains.

The Route

0.0 Paradise parking lot
0.2 Barn Flats

0.3 Devil's Dip
0.7 Paradise Road
1.0 Narada Falls

When the fog is so thick you'll swear somebody whitewashed your goggles, Devil's Dip is the place to go. Spot a car at Narada Falls and you can spend the day riding down and driving back up.

   The trail, sometimes marked by orange poles, has enough of a grade to allow you to get up close and personal with the trees. The technical term for this is "biting fir."

   Though none of the route could be described as steep, Devil's Dip itself can provide an interesting diversion for those who may be lulled into

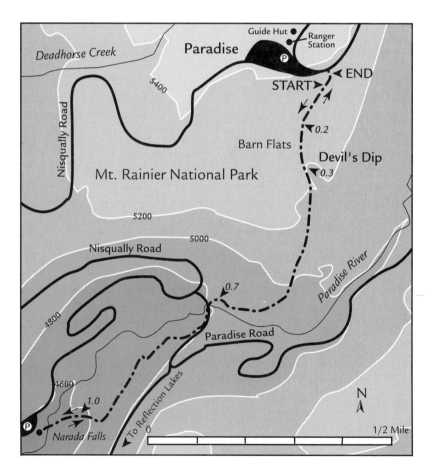

boredom by Barn Flats. Once so lulled, I crested the top of the dip—actually a steep gully with a rounded ridge on one side and a steeper, sharper ridge on the downhill side—and augered into the snow so deep that my companions were almost able to make one entire trip to Narada Falls and back before I could dig myself out.

Begin by skiing past the Paradise Inn on the Paradise Road, then turn south, or right, down a gully just before the road turns north above Paradise Valley. Boarders aren't likely to enjoy crossing Barn Flats and will have more fun riding the hills of Paradise Valley (Route 7).

Skiers with reckless abandon can schuss the gully, which opens onto Barn Flats. Skiers who wish to remain wreck-less may find that a few well-placed telemark turns will help control their speed.

Cross Barn Flats to the south where a second gully, Devil's Dip, drops steeply to the southeast. Cross the gully with a descending traverse and follow the trail (the widest opening in the trees) as it gradually turns to the southwest and, finally, west at about 4,900 feet.

At about 0.7 mile, the trail emerges from the forest and crosses the Paradise Road just before it joins the main road to Paradise. Turn left on the road and cross the bridge over Paradise River.

Just across the creek, pick up the trail to the right as it drops into the woods to the southwest and follow it to Narada Falls. There's a warming hut at Narada Falls, a good spot for lunch in bad weather.

11 | MOUNT RAINIER
Camp Muir

❄❄❄❄❄

Distance:	8.6 miles
Base elevation:	5,400 feet
Elevation gain:	4,800 feet
Trail time:	8 hours
Trail type:	Summer trail, backcountry
Skill level:	Advanced
Avalanche potential:	Considerable
Traction advisory:	Skins, waxless
Maps:	Green Trails 270S; USGS Mount Rainier East (7.5' series)

Getting There

From Seattle, drive south on I-5 to exit 127 near Tacoma, which leads to State Route 512 east. Once on SR 512, take the first exit, Steele Street, in order to bypass the heaviest traffic along SR 7 in Spanaway and Parkland. Follow Steele Street and Spanaway Loop Road around Parkland and Spanaway and turn south on SR 7 on the southern outskirts of Spanaway. Follow SR 7 south to Elbe, then follow SR 706 through Ashford to the Nisqually entrance to Mount Rainier National Park. Be prepared to pay a $10 per carload entrance fee to the park.

For information about snow and driving conditions inside the park, see the Getting There section for Route 1, Alta Vista.

Once at Paradise, drive 200 yards east of the Henry M. Jackson Visitor Center to the large parking lot. Rest rooms, a ranger station, and the Rainier Mountaineering, Inc., guide hut (closed in winter) are located here. Overnight parking is permitted in a section of the lot; ask a ranger.

Allow about three and a half hours from Seattle to Paradise. It will take longer if the gate is late in opening or you have to put on chains.

The Route

0.0 Paradise parking lot
1.0 Edith Basin saddle (Glacier Vista)

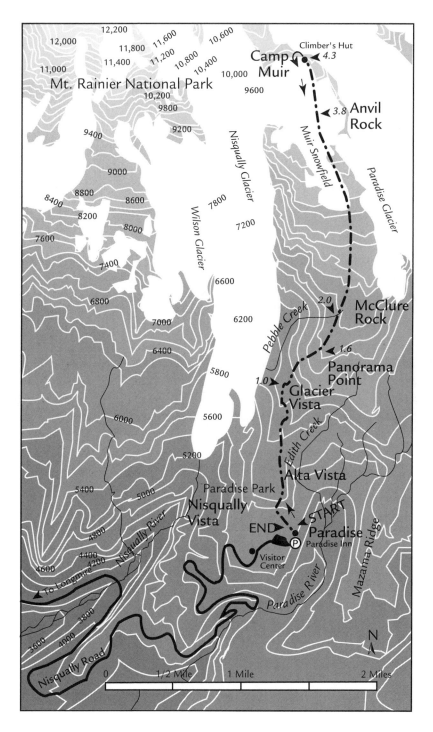

Mt. Rainier National Park

12,200
12,000
11,800   11,600
11,400   11,200   10,600
11,000   10,800   10,400
           10,200   10,000
9400   9800   9600
           9200
9000
8800   8600
8400
8200   8000
7600
                7800
7400   7200
6800   6600
7000
6400   6200
                5800
                5600
6000
5400   5000   5200
4800
4600   4400
4200
3600   3800
4000

Nisqually Glacier
Wilson Glacier
Muir Snowfield
Paradise Glacier
Pebble Creek
Edith Creek
Paradise Park
Mazama Ridge
Nisqually River
Paradise River

Camp Muir
Climber's Hut ◄ 4.3
▼
◄ 3.8 Anvil Rock
2.0 ▼
1.6 ◄ McClure Rock
1.0 ► Panorama Point
Glacier Vista
Alta Vista
Nisqually Vista
END ►START
Ⓟ Paradise
Paradise Inn
Visitor Center

To Longmire ◄
Nisqually Road

0   1/2 Mile   1 Mile   2 Miles

N

1.6   Panorama Point
2.0   Pebble Creek
3.8   Anvil Rock
4.3   Camp Muir

This is a most excellent adventure. Most snowriders climb to 10,080-foot Camp Muir in the late spring, summer, or fall. Winter southwesterlies scour the snow, packing it to frozen concrete. But rare, clear winter days after a dump of snow brought in by northerlies can make Muir some of the best backcountry skiing and boarding found anywhere in the state.

You'll catch 4,800 feet of vertical, with the opportunity—if your legs can stand it—to extend the journey another 1,700 vertical feet (see Route 12, Nisqually Glacier). While most of the hill is suitable for telemarkers with inter-mediate skill, the steep sections will test riders of all abilities. It isn't so much the grade of the hill that makes the Muir Snowfield such a great ride, but the fact that it goes on and on. And on.

Lungs and thighs accustomed to mile-high turns must now be ready to take on two-mile-high turns. You can quite literally turn until you drop. While dropped, take a moment to contemplate the view to the south: the Tatoosh Range in the near foreground, with Mount St. Helens off to the southwest and Adams off to the southeast. Between them, on the kind of clear winter days that bring snowriders to Muir, stands Mount Hood.

First, a word of caution: Unless your name is Jim, Lou, or Peter Whittaker, don't climb above Panorama Point if the weather sucks. There's little point in snowriding on the Muir Snowfield when you can't see, especially with so many inviting hills around Paradise. Experienced skiers have literally skied off cliffs they didn't see under whiteout conditions on the Muir Snowfield. At least one—Doug Vercoe in 1983—has never been found. If clouds appear or the wind picks up, turn around immediately.

Begin by following the trail to the Edith Creek saddle (described in Route 2, Panorama Point Loop). This route should be well tracked; if not, climb around the west side of Alta Vista at about 5,600 feet to the Deadhorse Creek drainage and follow it up to the base of Panorama Point, about 6,000 feet.

Two routes are possible from here. The first, directly up the south-facing ridge of Pan Point, is safest. This slope is marked by several trees about halfway up—the last trees you'll see—and is least likely to release if ava-lanche danger is moderate or higher.

A second route follows the summer trail by contouring around the base of Pan to the west, then switching back up the steep west face of this 6,920-foot promontory. This part of the route is the most dangerous in terms of avalanches. Once on top, the route flattens and even descends slightly to Pebble Creek.

The Muir Snowfield begins just above Pebble Creek. On the only days you belong there, you will feel the immensity of the place by looking up to the north more than two miles to Camp Muir, that black dot on the flat saddle below Gibraltar Rock. Climb past Anvil Rock, which will be to the east. Most of the hill is gentle enough to climb directly with skins without switching back.

At more than 10,000 feet above sea level, Camp Muir is not a place you'll want to linger in the winter, especially on the kind of clear, cold day that permits you to be here in midseason. Better to admire the view of the Cowlitz Glacier and Cathedral Rocks, then crank several hundred turns down to warm up enough for lunch.

12 MOUNT RAINIER
Nisqually Glacier
❄❄❄❄½

Distance:	2.6 miles one way
Base elevation:	5,400 feet
Elevation gain/loss:	900 feet/2,500 feet
Trail time:	5 hours one way
Trail type:	Summer trail, backcountry
Skill level:	Advanced
Avalanche potential:	Considerable
Traction advisory:	Skins, waxless
Maps:	Green Trails 270S; USGS Mount Rainier West, USGS Mount Rainier East (7.5' series)

Getting There

From Seattle, drive south on I-5 to exit 127 near Tacoma, which leads to State Route 512 east. Once on SR 512, take the first exit, Steele Street, in order to bypass the heaviest traffic along SR 7 in Spanaway and Parkland. Follow Steele Street and Spanaway Loop Road around Parkland and Spanaway and turn south on SR 7 on the southern outskirts of Spanaway. Follow SR 7 south to Elbe, then follow SR 706 through Ashford to the Nisqually entrance to Mount Rainier National Park. Be prepared to pay a $10 per carload entrance fee to the park.

For information about snow and driving conditions inside the park, see the Getting There section for Route 1, Alta Vista.

Once at Paradise, drive 200 yards east of the Henry M. Jackson Visitor Center to the large parking lot. Rest rooms, a ranger station, and the Rainier Mountaineering, Inc., guide hut (closed in winter) are located here. Overnight parking is permitted in a section of the lot; ask a ranger.

Allow about three and a half hours from Seattle to Paradise. It will take longer if the gate is late in opening or you have to put on chains.

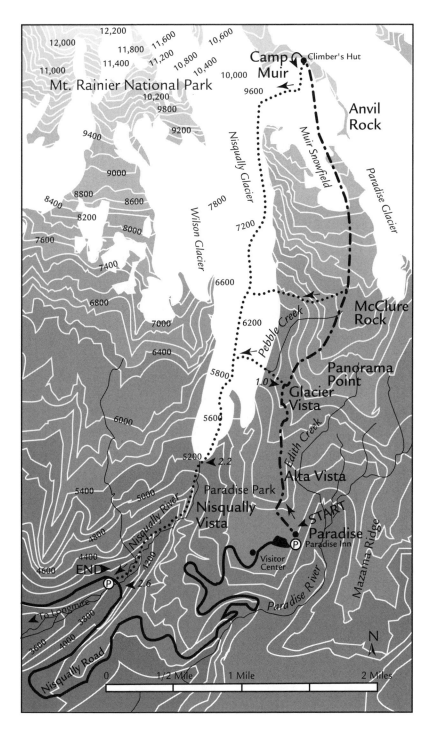

The Route

0.0 Paradise parking lot
1.0 Glacier Vista
2.2 Nisqually Glacier snout
2.6 Nisqually River bridge

Begin by following the summer trail to Edith Creek saddle (described in Route 2, Panorama Point Loop). Continue around the west side of Panorama Point to Glacier Vista, about 6,300 feet.

It's all downhill from here. From Glacier Vista, drop down onto the Nisqually Glacier, gaining the lateral moraine at about 6,000 feet. This first hill is a good ride and the base of the glacier a good turnaround spot when the weather or visibility is bad.

Once on the moraine, drop onto the glacier with a downhill traverse to the north or by plunging down the steep west face of the moraine onto the snow-covered ice at about 5,800 feet. Traverse downhill to the middle of the glacier, then turn down the broad icefield. Sags in the snow and snowdrifts make good spots for boarders.

Avoid this route in summer, when the glacier is scarred by hundreds of crevasses. The Nisqually is relatively safe for travel in winter, when bridges of snow 20 feet thick or more cover the cracks in the ice. Nonetheless, stay alert, and above all, don't ski into anything that looks like a big, bottomless hole in the snow. This is a route only for snowriders with advanced skills and with glacier travel experience.

As you near the snout of the glacier, the slope steepens considerably. Stay along the east side of the glacier, steering around a nunatak—a big rock that splits the glacier around it—to the east side. Here is the steepest part of the route (around 40 degrees) dropping about 200 feet to the spot where the Nisqually River claws its way out of the ice.

In winters of heavy snowfall, you can ski or ride the half mile to the Nisqually bridge and parking lot along the east side of the river. Boulders and sometimes avalanche debris from above are the primary worries in this section.

This route can be combined with the Camp Muir route for a long day and about 6,500 vertical feet of skiing. You should allow at least 12 hours for the attempt, making April a good month with enough daylight to try such an adventure.

13 MOUNT RAINIER
Castle Saddle
❊❊❊❊

Distance:	6.0 miles
Base elevation:	4,600 feet
Elevation gain:	1,600 feet
Trail time:	6 hours
Trail type:	Road, summer trail, backcountry
Skill level:	Advanced
Avalanche potential:	Considerable
Traction advisory:	Skins, waxless
Maps:	Green Trails 270S; USGS Mount Rainier East, USGS Packwood (7.5' series)

Castle Saddle is the flat snowfield at top, left.

Getting There

From Seattle, drive south on I-5 to exit 127 near Tacoma, which leads to State Route 512 east. Once on SR 512, take the first exit, Steele Street, in order to bypass the heaviest traffic along SR 7 in Spanaway and Parkland. Follow Steele Street and Spanaway Loop Road around Parkland and Spanaway and turn south on SR 7 on the southern outskirts of Spanaway. Follow SR 7 south to Elbe, then follow SR 706 through Ashford to the Nisqually entrance to Mount Rainier National Park. Be prepared to pay a $10 per carload entrance fee to the park.

For information about snow, driving conditions inside the park, and amenities at Paradise, see the Getting There section for Route 1, Alta Vista.

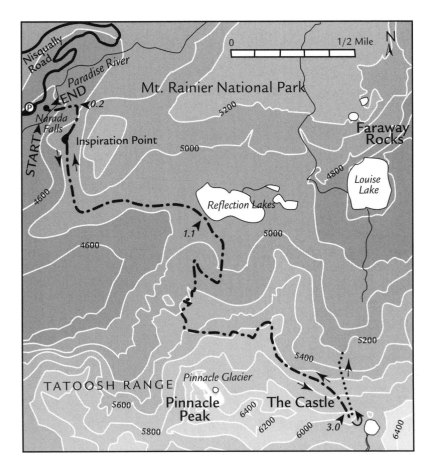

Park in the Narada Falls parking area, about 8 miles above Longmire on the Paradise Road.

Allow a little less than three and a half hours from Seattle to Narada Falls. It will take longer if the gate is late in opening or you have to put on chains.

The Route
0.0 Narada Falls parking area
0.2 Reflection Lakes Road
1.1 Reflection Lakes
3.0 Castle Saddle

Here's a good route to try in springtime, when you are searching for northern slopes with the possibility of lighter snow. From the 6,000-foot saddle just east of the Castle in the Tatoosh Range, you can become neurotic deciding which view to look at—Rainier to the north or St. Helens, Adams, and Hood to the south—or which side of the ridge to tackle—the north for better snow or the south for the omigodimdead steeps.

Begin by climbing the steep slope just east of the Narada Falls warming hut to the Reflection Lakes Road 240 feet above. Ski the road to Reflection Lakes.

Leave the road about a tenth of a mile past the east end of the first lake and climb south into a bowl, switching back to the northwest at about 5,100 feet. After climbing to about 5,200 feet, switchback again to the southeast and traverse across the slope at around 5,400 feet, crossing a wide ridge to the east below the Castle, the rocky block to the south.

Climb into a wide bowl east of the Castle. Ascend in a southerly traverse to the crest of the bowl, east of the Castle. The lowest part of this saddle may be corniced. The saddle makes a good lunch spot from which to yo-yo the bowl you've just climbed or the steeper south slope. (You can also climb southeast across an unnamed 6,524-foot peak to the Unicorn Glacier to ski or ride the south side of Unicorn, the 6,917-foot monarch of the Tatoosh Range.)

The best route down from the Castle saddle is to ride to the bottom of the bowl and follow your tracks. Cliff bands below 5,400 feet to the north can challenge expert skiers and riders.

14 West Side Road

½

Distance:	9.6 miles
Base elevation:	2,100 feet
Elevation gain:	1,500 feet
Trail time:	5 hours
Trail type:	Gravel road
Skill level:	Novice
Avalanche potential:	Low
Traction advisory:	Waxless
Maps:	Green Trails 269; USGS Mount Rainier National Park, Washington (1:50,000); Mount Wow, Randle (7.5' series)

Getting There

From Seattle, drive south on I-5 to exit 127 near Tacoma, which leads to State Route 512 east. Once on SR 512, take the first exit, Steele Street, in order to bypass the heaviest traffic along SR 7 in Spanaway and Parkland. Follow Steele Street and Spanaway Loop Road around Parkland and Spanaway and turn south on SR 7 on the southern outskirts of Spanaway. Follow SR 7 south to Elbe, then follow SR 706 through Ashford to the Nisqually entrance to Mount Rainier National Park. Be prepared to pay a $10 per carload entrance fee to the park.

For information about snow, driving conditions inside the park, and amenities at Paradise, see the Getting There section for Route 1, Alta Vista.

Drive 0.5 mile past the Nisqually entrance station to the West Side Road, turn left, and park along the road.

Allow a little less than three and a half hours from Seattle to West Side Road. It will take longer if the gate is late in opening or you have to put on chains.

The Route

0.0 Road gate
3.2 Fish Creek
4.8 Tahoma Vista

The West Side Road, which is gated at its intersection with the Paradise Road in winter, makes a fun outing for the entire family—even when there isn't any snow, as may be the case during some mild winters.

When the gravel road is covered with snow, it provides just enough of a grade to let you know you're climbing and a hill to give you a relaxing ride back to the car. For romance, ski the West Side Road on a moonlit night; for challenge, try it skiing backward, as a good friend of mine once did.

The road climbs gently for the first mile through the forest above Tahoma Creek, which wanders in braids below and to the east of the road. The steep ridge of Mount Wow stretches out of sight in the forest to the west.

Tributaries from the west have caused numerous washouts and slides. The biggest bites out of the road have been taken by Fish Creek, which sometimes

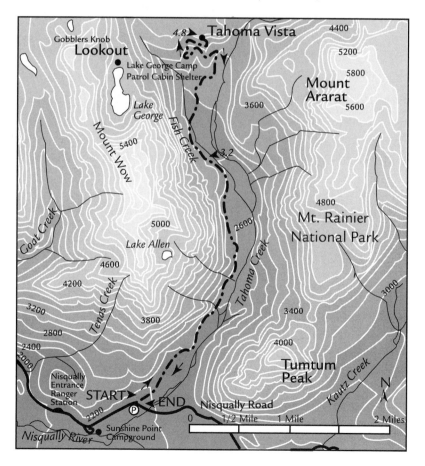

shares the road right-of-way. The road is closed completely to vehicles at about 3.2 miles, a good spot to turn around if you've got younger skiers in tow.

Beyond Fish Creek, the route climbs more steeply to the old Tahoma Creek campground, closed after repeated mudslides unleashed from the Tahoma Glacier convinced park officials that camping there wasn't such a good idea.

Past the old campground, the road turns east and climbs steeply up the ridge above Fish Creek. It switches back at about 3,200 feet and in about a half mile reaches Tahoma Vista, the turnaround spot.

Those seeking more exercise can continue following the old road up and down as it winds around the western flank of Mount Rainier. It once stretched more than 10 miles to the Puyallup River, where Wonderland Trail hikers now cross the river on a fine concrete bridge originally built for autos.

MOUNT RAINIER
Longmire Area

½

Distance:	0.5 to 3.2 miles
Base elevation:	2,700 feet
Elevation gain:	0 to 500 feet
Trail time:	30 minutes to 3 hours
Trail type:	Summer trail
Skill level:	Novice
Avalanche potential:	Low
Traction advisory:	Waxless, waxable
Maps:	Green Trails 269; USGS Mount Rainier National Park, Washington (1:50,000); Mount Rainier West (7.5' series)

Getting There

From Seattle, drive south on I-5 to exit 127 near Tacoma, which leads to State Route 512 east. Once on SR 512, take the first exit, Steele Street, in order to bypass the heaviest traffic along SR 7 in Spanaway and Parkland. Follow Steele Street and Spanaway Loop Road around Parkland and Spanaway and turn south on SR 7 on the southern outskirts of Spanaway. Follow SR 7 south to Elbe, then follow SR 706 through Ashford to the Nisqually entrance to Mount Rainier National Park. Be prepared to pay a $10 per carload entrance fee to the park.

For information about snow, driving conditions inside the park, and amenities at Paradise, see the Getting There section for Route 1, Alta Vista.

Park at the Longmire parking area, 7 miles up Paradise Road from the Nisqually entrance station.

Allow a little less than three and a half hours from Seattle to Longmire. It will take longer if the gate is late in opening or you have to put on chains.

The Route

0.0 Longmire parking area
1.6 Cougar Rock Campground

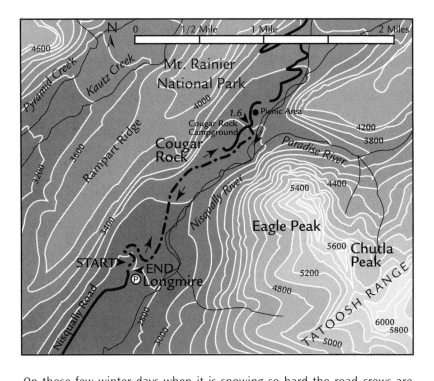

On those few winter days when it is snowing so hard the road crews are unable to open the road to Paradise, you can find places to ski around Longmire. One route is the trail just across the road from the Longmire Inn, a half-mile loop around Longmire Meadows.

A longer trail begins just past the gate on the road to Paradise at the first switchback and large parking area. This trail drops down along the Nisqually River and climbs gently along the river flats to the Cougar Rock Campground and picnic area. For more exercise, ski around the campground loop or picnic area.

Crystal Mountain/Highway 410

Hiding from the major storms in the lee of Mount Rainier, Crystal Mountain is arguably the state's finest lift-served winter-play area. Backcountry skiers and riders benefit from the same geography and, for most of the routes described here, owe their easy access to roads leading to the ski resort nearby.

Snow around the Crystal Mountain area is typical of most of the white stuff you'll find in the Cascades. It's not often fluffy and light, but what there is can be joyfully deep. And convenience to the Seattle area makes this a fine choice for backcountry snowriders with only a day to spend on the slopes.

Following is at least one route that may appeal to cross-country skiers and five hills for the steep-and-deep crowd.

16 CRYSTAL MOUNTAIN/HWY 410
Corral Pass

❄ ½

Distance:	12.0 miles
Base elevation:	2,700 feet
Elevation gain:	2,800 feet
Trail time:	7 hours
Trail type:	Forest road
Skill level:	Intermediate
Avalanche potential:	Low
Traction advisory:	Waxless, skins
Maps:	Green Trails 238, 239, 270; USGS Noble Knob, Sun Top, White River Park (7.5' series)

Getting There

From Seattle, drive south on I-5 to exit 149 and follow State Route 167 to Auburn (or take I-405 and SR 167 to Auburn). Exit at Auburn and follow SR 164 east about 15 miles to Enumclaw. Join SR 410 in Enumclaw and drive through Greenwater to Crystal Mountain Boulevard. Turn left at Crystal Mountain Boulevard and then right about 0.1 mile past the intersection into the Silver Creek Sno-Park. Allow about two hours to drive from Seattle.

The Route

0.0 Silver Creek Sno-Park
1.0 Corral Pass Road (Forest Road 7174)
3.5 Final switchback
4.8 Timberline
6.0 Corral Pass

You can work up a good lather on the moderately steep road to Corral Pass and get some hard-won thrills on the way down. While the telemark and snowplow are good techniques to know before embarking on this tour, a good butt-plant in precise strategic locations works just as well to control speed and keep fir facials to a minimum.

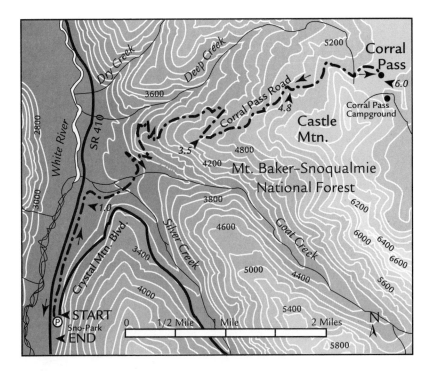

Begin by crossing Crystal Mountain Boulevard and skiing or walking north along SR 410, from whence you came, for about 1.0 mile to the Corral Pass Road on the right. The road climbs past several private recreational cabins before getting down (up) to the business of climbing a half mile into the clouds.

You'll climb through fir forest along the Coral Pass Road for almost 4 miles, switching back at least eight times before arriving at timberline around 5,200 feet. Continue climbing on the road about a quarter mile into a broad bowl formed by the 5,800-foot west ridge and the 6,400-foot north ridge of Castle Mountain. This bowl treats snowriders to good north-facing powder.

Cross-country skiers headed toward the pass can keep climbing to a second bowl at about 5,600 feet and finally, in another quarter mile, to the pass. To the south is a flat, snow-covered parking area, and beyond, a summer campground. To the north is Mutton Mountain and Dalles Ridge.

Just guess the name of that big, beautiful snow-covered thing to the west. Drink some water with your view and enjoy the ride home.

CRYSTAL MOUNTAIN/HWY 410
17 Bullion Basin

❄❄❄❄

Distance:	4.0 miles
Base elevation:	4,200 feet
Elevation gain:	2,000 feet
Trail time:	5 hours
Trail type:	Summer trail, backcountry
Skill level:	Intermediate
Avalanche potential:	Considerable
Traction advisory:	Skins, waxable
Maps:	Green Trails 271; USGS Norse Peak (7.5' series)

Bullion Basin, left, from Crystal Mountain.

Getting There

From Seattle, drive south on I-5 to exit 149 and follow State Route 167 to Auburn (or take I-405 and SR 167 to Auburn). Exit at Auburn and follow SR 164 about 15 miles to Enumclaw. Join SR 410 in Enumclaw and drive through Greenwater to Crystal Mountain Boulevard. Turn left at Crystal Mountain Boulevard and then right, past the intersection of the Silver Creek Sno-Park, to the Crystal Mountain Resort. Allow about two hours to drive from Seattle.

The Route

0.0   Crystal Mountain parking area
0.4   Bullion Basin trailhead
0.8   Steep, open slopes
1.5   Bullion Basin
2.0   Pacific Crest Trail

Snowriding in Bullion Basin is one of the most convenient ways to get a back-country downhill rush. You'll find a steep, north-facing ride through trees, a more gentle and open southern slope, and views along the crest of the ridge that should be patented by the Washington tourism bureau.

The basin and slopes above can be reached by snowriders who have only half a day. The route is especially convenient to boarders who are snow-shoeing or postholing because they won't waste any energy traversing. (If you have more time, follow the route past Bullion Basin to Cement and Lake Basins beyond, Routes 18 and 19.)

From the upper parking area, climb along the extreme left side of the handle tow in the children's ski area east of the Crystal Mountain chapel to a road that climbs north through the trees at about 4,800 feet. Follow this road as it climbs to the Bullion Basin summer trailhead where, depending upon snow depth, you may find a sign.

The route follows the summer trail, which climbs on a traverse to the north for about 0.4 mile, crossing the creek that drains Bullion Basin. The trail breaks into steep, open hillside at about 5,000 feet, then switches back after a tenth of a mile to reenter the trees.

Continue switching back along the tree line, keeping the steep creek gully below you on the right. Climb into the bottom of Bullion Basin by making a climbing traverse to the south at about 5,600 feet. Depending upon your climbing skins and aerobic capacity, the 6,200-foot saddle at the southeast

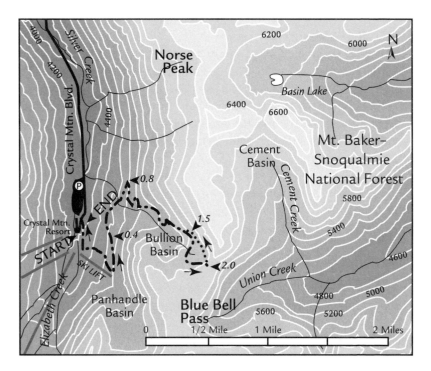

head of the basin is about a half mile away and the Pacific Crest Trail is just on the other side of the saddle.

You can descend from any spot along the ridge above the basin, but avoid the south-facing slope if avalanche danger is moderate or considerable. This slope is the most likely to slide of any surrounding the basin but is a good downhill run when conditions permit.

The easiest route back is to follow your tracks up, cutting switchbacks whenever possible.

18 | CRYSTAL MOUNTAIN/HWY 410
Cement Basin
❄❄❄❄

Distance: 6.8 miles
Base elevation: 4,200 feet
Elevation gain: 2,500 feet
Trail time: 6 hours
Trail type: Summer trail, backcountry
Skill level: Advanced
Avalanche potential: Considerable
Traction advisory: Skins, waxable
Maps: Green Trails 271; USGS Norse Peak (7.5' series)

Getting There

From Seattle, drive south on I-5 to exit 149 and follow State Route 167 to Auburn (or take I-405 and SR 167 to Auburn). Exit at Auburn and follow SR 164 about 15 miles to Enumclaw. Join SR 410 in Enumclaw and drive through Greenwater to Crystal Mountain Boulevard. Turn left at Crystal Mountain Boulevard and then right, past the intersection for the Silver Creek Sno-Park, to the Crystal Mountain Resort. Allow about two hours to drive from Seattle.

The Route

0.0 Crystal Mountain parking area
2.0 Pacific Crest Trail
2.7 6,700-foot peak
3.4 Cement Basin

This is the second of three basins along the summit of the Pacific Crest Trail that make for an excellent backcountry adventure convenient to all the civilized amenities of Crystal Mountain. You can climb up in the morning, ride or ski all day, and jump in the hot tub before heading home.

Follow Route 17 (Bullion Basin) to the 6,200-foot ridge crest above Bullion Basin, then turn northeast along the crest of the ridge. Climb up and over the 6,700-foot knoll, keeping west of the ridge to avoid possible cornices.

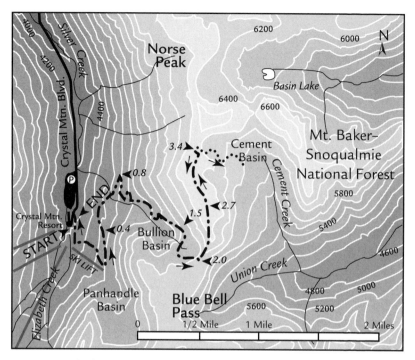

Drop to the low point on this ridge at about 6,500 feet. Cement Basin is the open bowl directly east of this saddle. You can make runs to the east of about 450 vertical feet without biting fir.

Save enough energy for the climb back and the run down Bullion Basin.

19 CRYSTAL MOUNTAIN/HWY 410
Lake Basin
❋❋❋❋

Distance: 8.8 miles
Base elevation: 4,200 feet
Elevation gain: 2,500 feet
Trail time: 7 hours
Trail type: Summer trail, backcountry
Skill level: Advanced
Avalanche potential: Considerable
Traction advisory: Skins, waxless
Maps: Green Trails 271; USGS Norse Peak
(7.5' series)

Getting There

From Seattle, drive south on I-5 to exit 149 and follow State Route 167 to Auburn (or take I-405 and SR 167 to Auburn). Exit at Auburn and follow SR 164 about 15 miles to Enumclaw. Join SR 410 in Enumclaw and drive through Greenwater to Crystal Mountain Boulevard. Turn left at Crystal Mountain Boulevard and then right, past the intersection for the Silver Creek Sno-Park, to the Crystal Mountain Resort. Allow about two hours to drive from Seattle.

The Route

0.0 Crystal Mountain parking area
3.4 Cement Basin
4.4 Scout Pass

Yet a third powder-laden bowl awaits strong skiers and boarders climbing from the Crystal Mountain parking area. To get there, climb over the 6,720-foot peak just north of Cement Basin (see Route 18) and descend to the low point at about 6,600 feet, called Scout Pass.

The bowl immediately east of this saddle is Lake Basin—possibly so named because there is a lake in the basin named Basin Lake. Or perhaps Basin Lake was so named because the basin in which the lake is located is named Lake Basin.

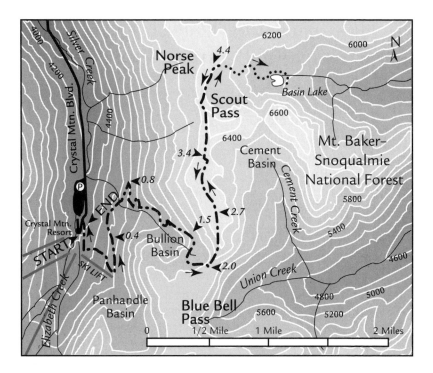

Never mind. Have a nice day. You'll get around 700 vertical feet if you rip all the way down to the lake.

(Yet another bowl—Big Crow Basin—can be found on the north side of neighboring 6,856-foot Norse Peak, about 0.75 mile away. This bowl can be reached by climbing north over Norse Peak, but only the strongest and fastest snowriders will have any time left for more than one or two runs.)

20 CRYSTAL MOUNTAIN/HWY 410
Silver Basin
❄❄❄❄

Distance:	4.4 miles
Base elevation:	4,200 feet
Elevation gain:	2,400 feet
Trail time:	4.5 hours
Trail type:	Ski run, backcountry
Skill level:	Intermediate
Avalanche potential:	Moderate
Traction advisory:	Skins, waxable
Maps:	Green Trails 270, 271; USGS Norse Peak (7.5' series)

Hen Skin Lake, with Silver Basin in background. Note split board.

Getting There

From Seattle, drive south on I-5 to exit 149 and follow State Route 167 to Auburn (or take I-405 and SR 167 to Auburn). Exit at Auburn and follow SR 164 about 15 miles to Enumclaw. Join SR 410 in Enumclaw and drive through Greenwater to Crystal Mountain Boulevard. Turn left at Crystal Mountain Boulevard and then right, past the intersection of the Silver Creek Sno-Park, to the Crystal Mountain Resort. Allow about two hours to drive from Seattle.

The Route

0.0 Crystal Mountain parking area
1.0 Top of Chair 4
1.2 Hen Skin Lake
2.2 Silver King saddle

Silver Basin is within the boundaries of the designated backcountry of Crystal Mountain Resort. For this reason, backcountry snowriders bound for Silver Basin or Crystal Basin beyond should check and may be asked to register with

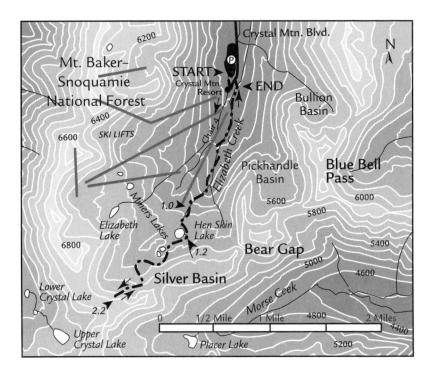

the Crystal Mountain Ski Patrol. Patrollers can give you the latest information on avalanche danger and provide valuable advice on finding the best snow.

When conditions are right, you can climb to the summit of 7,012-foot Silver King for a 1,200-vertical-foot ride to the trees at the bottom of the basin. Snow on this northeast-facing slope is usually light and deep and often causes a malady that strikes snowriders on sunny, powder-filled days. The medical term for this ailment is "yahoo syndrome."

From the parking area, climb south-southwest up the beginner's run under Chair 4 at Crystal. Stay as far off the ski run as possible; skiers with good skins can probably climb directly along the tree line.

To avoid most downhill skiers, you can follow a run in the woods east of the lift, identified as Boondoggle. This run enters the woods at the halfway station on Chair 4 and exits at the top of the lift.

From the top of the lift, follow a packed and groomed trail into the woods south of the lift for about a quarter mile to Hen Skin Lake. Climb around the west shore of the lake and turn southwest at the south end to Miners Lakes at 5,600 feet.

Cross a forested ridge west of Miners Lakes and climb southwest to the saddle between Silver King, on the right, and 6,796-foot Three-Way Peak on the left. If conditions permit, climb the ridge to the summit of Silver King.

The run down from either the saddle or the summit should be into Silver Basin. The bowl to the north of Silver King is called Avalanche Basin, for reasons you would be wise not to investigate.

21 Crystal Basin

❄❄❄❄½

Distance:	4.4 miles
Base elevation:	4,200 feet
Elevation gain:	2,400 feet
Trail time:	4.5 hours
Trail type:	Ski run, backcountry
Skill level:	Advanced
Avalanche potential:	Moderate
Traction advisory:	Skins, waxable
Maps:	Green Trails 270, 271; USGS Norse Peak, White River Park (7.5' series)

Cornices above Crystal Basin make good launch pads.

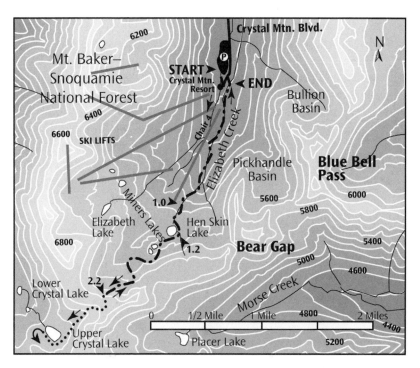

Getting There

From Seattle, drive south on I-5 to exit 149 and follow State Route 167 to Auburn (or take I-405 and SR 167 to Auburn). Exit at Auburn and follow SR 164 about 15 miles to Enumclaw. Join SR 410 in Enumclaw and drive through Greenwater to Crystal Mountain Boulevard. Turn left at Crystal Mountain Boulevard and then right, past the intersection for the Silver Creek Sno-Park, to the Crystal Mountain Resort. Allow about two hours to drive from Seattle.

The Route

0.0 Crystal Mountain parking area
2.2 Silver King saddle

Crystal Basin is a fine sunset-facing bowl that treats riders and skiers to about 800 vertical feet of snow play on the steep, wild side. The white stuff here is more often subject to winds and winter sunshine; when Silver Basin offers good springtime powder, Crystal Basin on the opposite side of the ridge might yield sweet corn.

Follow the way described in Route 20, Silver Basin, to the crest of the saddle between Silver King and Three-Way Peak. The fun begins here, when you drop off the saddle to the southwest into the basin holding Crystal Lake. The ridge crest is the boundary between Crystal Mountain Resort backcountry and Mount Rainier National Park.

You may find that a broad humpback ridge tumbling into the lake will be crusty or wind-packed, while snowriding on either side offers better snow.

To return, climb back to the Silver King saddle and ride down into Silver Basin. A summer trail leads from Crystal Lake to the northwest and State Route 410—at a point that is closed in the winter—and this can provide an alternative exit. But it's not recommended because of the thick forest that must be navigated and the two-mile ski down the highway to Crystal Mountain Boulevard.

22 CRYSTAL MOUNTAIN/HWY 410
Bear Gap
❄❄❄½

Distance: 4.0 miles
Base elevation: 4,200 feet
Elevation gain: 1,700 feet
Trail time: 3.5 hours
Trail type: Ski run, backcountry
Skill level: Intermediate
Avalanche potential: Moderate
Traction advisory: Skins, waxable
Maps: Green Trails 271; USGS Norse Peak
(7.5' series)

Bear Gap lies below the sharp peak at left.

Getting There

From Seattle, drive south on I-5 to exit 149 and follow State Route 167 to Auburn (or take I-405 and SR 167 to Auburn). Exit at Auburn and follow SR 164 about 15 miles to Enumclaw. Join SR 410 in Enumclaw and drive through Greenwater to Crystal Mountain Boulevard. Turn left at Crystal Mountain Boulevard and then right, past the intersection for the Silver Creek Sno-Park, to the Crystal Mountain Resort. Allow about two hours to drive from Seattle.

The Route

0.0 Crystal Mountain parking area
1.2 Hen Skin Lake
2.0 Bear Gap

The north side of this bowl is a sheltered collector of powder snow, which it keeps shaded and hidden from nasty warm winds and sunshine. If light snow exists anywhere in the Crystal backcountry, the gentle north slopes of Bear Gap are where you'll find it.

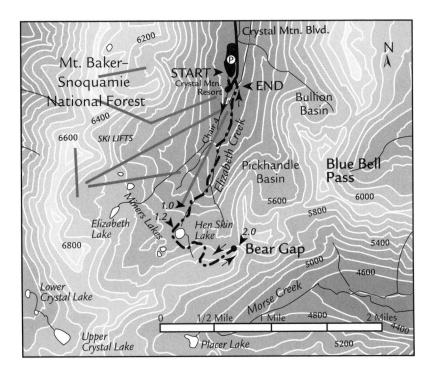

Follow the way described in Route 20, Silver Basin, to Hen Skin Lake. From the west shore of the lake, climb east-southeast to the low notch in the ridge at about 5,900 feet, Bear Gap. Yo-yo riding and skiing are possible through glades to the north for about 200 vertical feet before you must play tag with the fir trees.

A longer run is possible, when conditions permit, by riding the steep, open south slopes down to Morse Creek. From Bear Gap, traverse the south side of the ridge at the 5,800-foot level to the east until the slope opens below. You can ride almost to the end of the Morse Creek Road at 4,900 feet on open slopes.

Snow on the south side is likely to be consolidated by wind and sun, and snowriding on this side is probably best in the spring.

White Pass

Because of its geography—a vanguard of Cascade mountains and foothills to the southeast—and its 4,500-foot altitude, the White Pass area is an excellent choice for backcountry snowriders and cross-country skiers. The snow is likely to be drier, although we all know that in the Cascades, "dry" is a distinctly relative term.

Here you'll find five hills or routes with everything from a lift-served backcountry slope to a 5-mile road ski with great views. Snowriders might choose Hogback, Round Mountain, or the slope above Forest Road 1284 for the most fun; cross-country skiers might sample FR 1284 or the Tieton River Road. Sand Lake makes a great backcountry tour with a little bit of everything.

23 | WHITE PASS
Forest Road 1284

❄❄❄❄

Distance:	Telemark skiers, snowboard riders—1.0 mile; cross-country tour—6.6 miles
Base elevation:	4,320 feet
Elevation gain:	Tele-riders—720 feet; tour—380 feet
Trail time:	Tour—3.5 hours
Trail type:	Logging road
Skill level:	Tele-riders—intermediate to expert; tour—novice
Avalanche potential:	Tele-riders—considerable; tour—low
Traction advisory:	Tele-riders—skins or snowshoes; tour—waxable, waxless
Maps:	Green Trails 303; USGS White Pass (7.5' series)

Touring along Forest Road 1284.

Getting There

From Seattle, take I-5 south to exit 127, near Tacoma, which leads to State Route 512 east. In about a third of a mile, take the Steele Street exit off SR 512 in order to bypass the heaviest traffic along SR 7 in Spanaway and Parkland. Follow Steele Street and Spanaway Loop Road around Parkland and Spanaway and turn south on SR 7 on the southern outskirts of Spanaway. Follow SR 7 south to Elbe and Morton, then follow SR 12 east to White Pass.

Forest Road 1284 enters SR 12 from the north about a quarter mile west of the White Pass ski area. Turn left and follow 1284 about a tenth of a mile to a wide parking area next to a Department of Transportation equipment shed. The road is well maintained in the winter.

Allow about three and a half hours from Seattle, and longer if you must stop to put on chains.

The Route

0.0 Parking area
0.5 Downhill snowriders turn right for hill

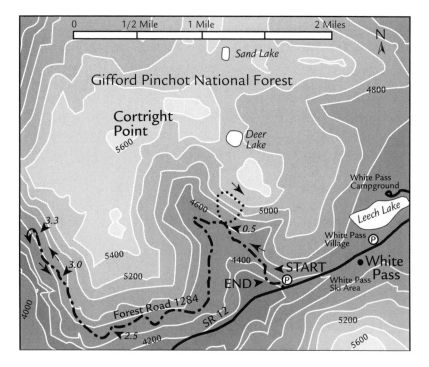

2.5 Sand Lake trailhead
3.0 Final clear-cut
3.3 Road ends at top of clear-cut

Telemarkers, randonee skiers, and boarders will find a sweet sunset-facing hill of about 720 vertical feet after only a half-mile trudge up the road. If you want steep wild snow convenient to civilization, this hill is tough to beat.

Climb from the road to the right, switching back up the clear-cut to the crest of the unnamed 5,360-foot peak on the northeast side of White Pass. You'll likely find the best turns down the southeast side of the clear-cut, to the right of your switchbacks.

Riders and skiers testing this slope can also cross the flat summit of the peak to the east and find a wide, open slope above Leech Lake. Since White Pass and Leech Lake are about 160 feet higher than the trailhead, the Leech Lake side yields only 560 feet of vertical. The north end of this slope is more open; remnants of an old ski jump can be seen above Leech Lake at the southern end.

Families and those who enjoy gentle touring should kick and glide below the hill, pausing long enough to wonder why anyone would want to climb up there in the first place. The road traverses gently above the White Pass Highway (SR 12) and the Millridge Creek basin for another 2.8 miles.

You'll stride through silent forests of Douglas fir decorated like Christmas trees with strands of green lichens. You'll cross through at least three clear-cuts tangled with 10- to 15-year-old evergreens just high enough that, if you decide to try a few telemark turns, you'll climb back to the road reeking of fir perfume.

The road crosses a creek culvert and climbs ever so gently through a clear-cut where views open to the south of the White Pass ski slopes and Hogback Ridge. As the road rounds a side ridge at about 2 miles, the view expands to the steeps to the west, above Knuppenburg Lake.

At 2.5 miles, skiers pass the Sand Lake trailhead. (This trail climbs steeply through heavy forest; to get to Sand Lake, it's better to take the approach described in Route 24, Sand Lake.)

A gentle climb leads another half mile to the final clear-cut where—if Mother Nature cooperates—you'll get a splendid view of Mount Rainier. This clear-cut is probably the best spot for practicing telemark turns, but the juvenile evergreens make it tough for wide-open skiing.

The road climbs along the top of the clear-cut and ends at the edge of the forest, about 4,700 feet. Here you'll find several large stump thrones to sit on while admiring the view.

24 | WHITE PASS
Sand Lake
❄❄

Distance:	5.6 miles, tour
Base elevation:	4,480 feet
Elevation gain:	820 feet
Trail time:	4 hours
Trail type:	Hiking trail
Skill level:	Intermediate
Avalanche potential:	Low
Traction advisory:	Waxless
Maps:	Green Trails 303; USGS White Pass (7.5' series)

Near the Sand Lake trailhead.

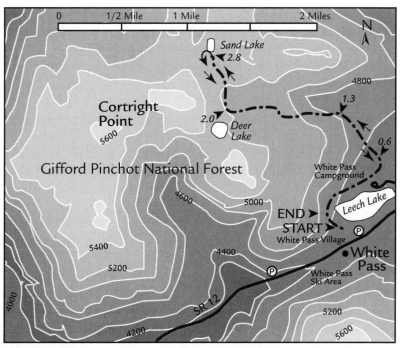

Getting There

From Seattle, take I-5 south to exit 127, near Tacoma, which leads to State Route 512 east. In about a third of a mile, take the Steele Street exit off SR 512 in order to bypass the heaviest traffic along SR 7 in Spanaway and Parkland. Follow Steele Street and Spanaway Loop Road around Parkland and Spanaway and turn south on SR 7 on the southern outskirts of Spanaway. Follow SR 7 south to Elbe and Morton, then follow SR 12 east (a quarter mile east of its intersection with Forest Road 1284) to the White Pass ski area.

Allow about three and a half hours from Seattle, and longer if you must stop to put on chains.

The Route

0.0 White Pass parking area
0.1 Leech Lake
0.6 Pacific Crest Trail junction; climb left
1.3 Trail 1107 junction; turn left
2.0 Deer Lake; turn right
2.8 Sand Lake

Telemarkers and riders will find the short, wide-open slope at the west end of Leech Lake to be the steepest and best along this tour. Switchback up the northerly end of this slope for about 560 vertical feet of downhill.

For the tour, ski past the White Pass parking area on the north side of the road and stay to the west of the White Pass Village Inn, traversing the western and northern slopes above Leech Lake. This part of the route follows the developed White Pass cross-country trail system, and backcountry skiers should make their own track above the groomed trail or pay the trail fee.

At the eastern end of the lake, look for signs of the Pacific Crest Trail and the White Pass trail system's Dark Meadows Loop climbing to the left. Turn left, above the developed trail, and follow this route through forest as it climbs to about 4,500 feet and joins with Trail 1107 from Dog Lake.

Turn left here (the developed trail turns right) and climb up the bowl formed by the creek draining Deer Lake. This route is the steepest part and passes several small meadows before crossing the snow-covered creek draining Deer Lake, a little less than half a mile from the trail junction. Climb another third of a mile to the shallow 5,200-foot basin holding Deer Lake.

On reaching the lake, turn right and climb a gentle slope to the north to Sand Lake. It's about three-quarters of a mile and 100 vertical feet from Deer Lake to Sand Lake.

25 WHITE PASS
Hogback Ridge
❄❄❄❄

Distance:	3.5 miles (lift); 6.0 miles (trail)
Base elevation:	6,000 feet (lift); 4,480 feet (trail)
Elevation gain:	840 feet (lift); 2,040 (trail)
Trail time:	Tour—4 hours
Trail type:	Cat track, off-trail
Skill level:	Telemark skiers, snowboard riders— advanced to expert; cross-country tour— intermediate
Avalanche potential:	Tele-riders—high; tour—low
Traction advisory:	Tele-riders—skins or snowshoes; tour— skins or waxless
Maps:	Green Trails 303; USGS White Pass, Old Snowy (7.5' series)

Getting There

From Seattle, take I-5 south to exit 127, near Tacoma, which leads to State Route 512 east. In about a third of a mile, take the Steele Street exit off SR 512 in order to bypass the heaviest traffic along SR 7 in Spanaway and Parkland. Follow Steele Street and Spanaway Loop Road around Parkland and Spanaway and turn south on SR 7 on the southern outskirts of Spanaway.

Fresh tracks in the basin below Hogback Ridge.

Follow SR 7 south to Elbe and Morton, then follow SR 12 east (a quarter mile east of its intersection with Forest Road 1284) to the White Pass ski area.

Allow about three and a half hours from Seattle, and longer if you must stop to put on chains.

The Route

0.0 White Pass parking area
0.4 Waterfall run; keep right
0.6 Cat track junction; switchback to the left
1.2 Chair 4
1.6 Hogback Meadows
2.1 Pacific Crest Trail route; climb right on ridge
3.0 Hogback Mountain summit

Excellent runs of 800 vertical feet or more on some of the best snow in the Cascades wait for you in the bowls of Hogback Mountain, an easy day outing—especially if you ride the Great White express lift. Those who hold to the Puritan work ethic can salve their consciences with sweat and climb from the White Pass lodge.

If riding the lift, ski or ride off Pigtail Peak to the south about 100 yards to the flat ridge crest at the ski area boundary. Follow this ridge crest about 1.7 miles to the southwest to Hogback Mountain.

Ski tourers and those planning to earn their turns can climb past the White Pass day lodge and travel west to the broad, flat cat track called Paradise. This is part of a developed ski run, and cross-country skiers should keep to the extreme right, or downhill side, of the track.

After passing the steep Waterfall ski run, you'll come to a junction in the cat track at about 0.6 mile. Ignore the temptation to stay on the flatter track to the right. This leads to a steep ski run.

Instead, switchback to the left, keeping to the extreme left of the trail. Skins will be a big help in this section and the steep, but short section that follows at the top of the Waterfall ski run, called Main Street.

The cat track flattens enough that those with waxless skis can climb. At 1.2 miles, you'll pass below Chair 4 and climb a short, steeper pitch at the bottom of the Quail ski run. After about 100 yards, angle to the right off the ski run. This is the ski area boundary.

You'll now enter a broad, flat basin that makes excellent touring on alpine meadow and fir glades. Part of this gentle Hogback Meadows is included in a 300-acre ski area expansion proposal.

The steeper Hogback Ridge is to the southwest. Continue climbing southerly until you reach the crest of the flat ridge at about 5,800 feet. Here, the Pacific Crest Trail will be about eight feet underneath the snow.

Turn southwest along the ridge crest and break out onto the alpine slopes of Hogback Mountain at 6,000 feet. Switchback up the ridge, climbing about 640 feet to the summit. The steepest bowl is east-southeast from the summit, swooping down to tiny Miriam Lake. As is too often the case, this hill also packs the greatest avalanche potential.

The bowl to the north of the summit is gentler and is a good hill to see if you can fry your thighs from too many turns. By virtue of its geography, the northerly bowl also is likely to hold good snow longer.

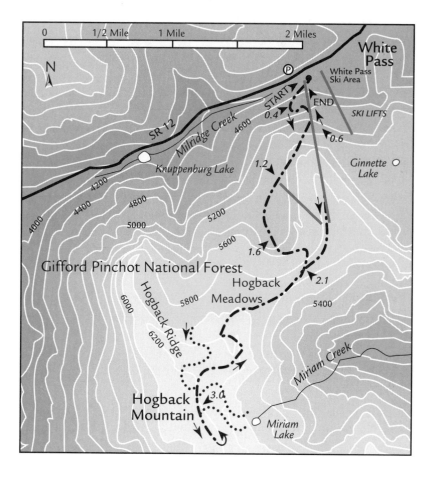

26 | North Fork Tieton River

❋❋

Distance:	9.8 miles
Base elevation:	3,040 feet
Elevation gain:	320 feet
Trail time:	5.5 hours
Trail type:	Forest road
Skill level:	Novice
Avalanche potential:	Low
Traction advisory:	Waxless, waxable skis
Maps:	Green Trails 303; USGS White Pass (7.5' series)

Getting There

From Seattle, take I-5 south to exit 127, near Tacoma, which leads to State Route 512 east. In about a third of a mile, take the Steele Street exit off SR 512 in order to bypass the heaviest traffic along SR 7 in Spanaway and Parkland. Follow Steele Street and Spanaway Loop Road around Parkland and Spanaway and turn south on SR 7 on the southern outskirts of Spanaway. Follow SR 7 south to Elbe and Morton, then follow SR 12 east past the White Pass ski area 7.5 miles to the Clear Lake Road (Forest Road 1200); turn right and follow it for 3 miles to the Tieton River Sno-Park—at FR 1207.

Allow about three and a half hours from Seattle, and longer if you must stop to put on chains.

The Route

0.0	Tieton River Sno-Park
1.4	Hell Creek crossing
2.5	Miriam Creek crossing
4.8	Scatter Creek crossing, Goat Rocks Wilderness
4.9	Tieton camp

Steep forested or clear-cut canyon walls on either side of the north fork of the Tieton River are the best bet for downhill thrills and spills on this tour. For a more exhilarating ride in this same area, try Route 27, Round Mountain.

Those looking for a good kick-and-glide with a fantastic view of the Goat Rocks Wilderness and 7,930-foot Old Snowy Mountain at the end must work for it. Novices and families will enjoy all or part of gentle Forest Road 1207 through forest and occasional meadow to summer trailheads leading to the heart of one of the Cascades' most splendid wilderness areas.

The road follows the river corridor and a half-mile-wide part of the valley carved by the Tieton River that is excluded from the Goat Rocks Wilderness. Tourers will drop gently to cross Hell Creek before beginning another gentle ascent to Miriam Creek.

The Tieton Valley stretches east to Rimrock Lake.

Just past Miriam Creek, the view up the valley opens and Old Snowy and the McCall Glacier fill the horizon. Old Snowy is a popular summer skiing area after Forest Service roads open.

Follow the road alternately through stands of second-growth evergreens and clear-cut areas to the loop parking area at the Goat Rocks Wilderness boundary. Skiers with another half-mile worth of energy might continue up the valley for a better view.

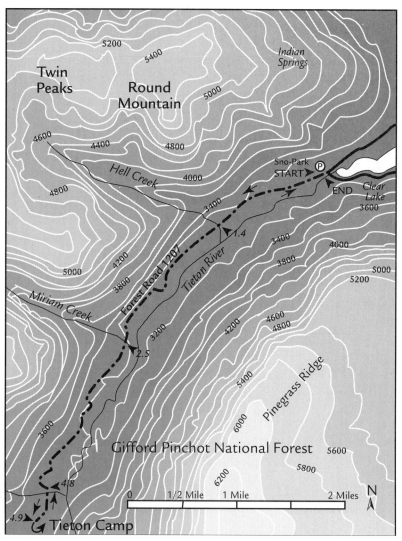

27 WHITE PASS
Round Mountain
❄❄❄❄

Distance:	Telemark skiers, snowboard riders—6.0 miles; cross-country tour—8.8 miles
Base elevation:	3,040 feet
Elevation gain:	Tele-riders—2,930 feet; tour—1,280 feet
Trail time:	Tele-riders—4 hours; tour—6 hours
Trail type:	Tele-riders—backcountry; tour—Forest road
Skill level:	Tele-riders—advanced; tour—intermediate
Avalanche potential:	Considerable
Traction advisory:	Tele-riders—skins, snowshoes; tour—waxless or waxable
Maps:	Green Trails 303; USGS White Pass (7.5' series)

Getting There

From Seattle, take I-5 south to exit 127, near Tacoma, which leads to State Route 512 east. In about a third of a mile, take the Steele Street exit off SR 512 in order to bypass the heaviest traffic along SR 7 in Spanaway and Parkland. Follow Steele Street and Spanaway Loop Road around Parkland and Spanaway and turn south on SR 7 on the southern outskirts of Spanaway. Follow SR 7 south to Elbe and Morton, then follow SR 12 east past the White Pass ski area 7.5 miles to the Clear Lake Road (Forest Road 1200); turn right

Skier at White Pass looking over at Round Mountain.

and follow it for 3 miles to the Tieton River Sno-Park—at FR 1207. Park in the Tieton River Sno-Park and ski back above FR 1200 for a fifth of a mile to FR 830. Both the downhill and tour routes start up FR 830.

Allow about three and a half hours from Seattle, and longer if you must stop to put on chains.

The Beginning Route

0.0 Tieton River Sno-Park
0.2 Forest Road 830; turn left
0.6 Junction with Forest Road 831; downhillers follow FR 831, tour skiers switchback on FR 830

Downhill Route

1.6 Forest Road 831 ends; switchback up northwest through forest to rejoin FR 830
1.9 Round Mountain summer trailhead on FR 830; climb west to the summit
3.0 Round Mountain summit

Tour Route

2.2 Switchback, Forest Road 830
3.4 Gully (potential avalanche danger)
4.0 Round Mountain summer trailhead on FR 830
4.4 FR 830 ends

Prepare for some serious cranking. Nearly 3,000 vertical feet of turning through trees—remember, ski or ride the openings, not the trees—and wide-open upper slopes should give you substantial aerobic challenge.

Although downhillers bound for the summit of 5,970-foot Round Mountain can simply climb up through the woods from the Sno-Park, a kinder, gentler route is to follow Forest Road 830 to FR 831, then climb on FR 831 to its end at 3,760 feet.

Switchback northwest up through the woods and a clear-cut area, keeping a steep gully to your left. You'll rejoin FR 830 at about 4,200 feet, about a third of a mile southwest of the summer trailhead to Round Mountain. Ski up the road to the trailhead, then switchback to the west up a wide, forested ridge to open slopes at 5,000 feet.

Continue climbing west for another 400 vertical feet to the summit ridge. Turn and climb southwest to the summit, once the site of a fire lookout.

The open, northeast-facing ridge you climbed provides the longest alpine run, while the drop-off to the north-northwest is likely to provide the best snow. The view to the southwest to Tieton Peak and Bear Creek Mountain will melt your mind.

Round Mountain is one of those places you might wish were easier to reach. But of course if it were, its glory might be diminished.

The tour route up FR 830 is straightforward, passing through dense woods and a few open spots with peekaboo views of the Goat Rocks Wilderness. While the road is never steep, it climbs sufficiently that cross-country skiers with the right wax should enjoy the ride down.

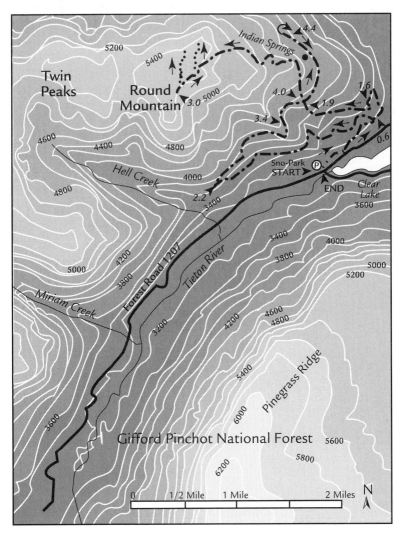

Mount St. Helens

May 18, 1980, was not only a historic day for geologists, but also for back-country skiers (this was back in the days when snowboards had wheels). Skiers on Mount Rainier that perfect sunny day were disappointed to find that a gray coating of ash on their corn snow did little to increase their speed.

Aside from that, the years following the eruption of Mount St. Helens opened up the relatively unexplored south side of the mountain with a different climbing route and no less than a mile of vertical snowriding on sunshine slopes. On sunny spring days, climb to the 8,200-foot south rim of this slumbering white giant and turn your legs to rubber flying back down.

In good winters, cross-country skiers looking for more gentle slopes and scenic tours will find them on lower benches and meadows on the south side of the mountain. The friendly folks of the Gifford Pinchot National Forest have done a good job of providing opportunities for winter fun for both snowriders and snowmobilers in this area.

28 MOUNT ST. HELENS
June Lake
❄

Distance:	4.8 miles
Base elevation:	2,600 feet
Elevation gain:	600 feet
Trail time:	4 hours
Trail type:	Forest road, summer trail
Skill level:	Intermediate
Avalanche potential:	Low
Traction advisory:	Waxable, waxless
Maps:	Green Trails 354S; USGS Mount St. Helens (7.5' series)

Getting There

From I-5 at Woodland, about 115 miles south of Tacoma, take exit 21 and follow State Route 503 east through Cougar to Forest Road 83. Follow FR 83 to the Marble Mountain Sno-Park (designated Cougar Sno-Park on the 1997–98 Washington Cross Country Ski Sno-Park pamphlet). Allow about three and a half hours travel time from Seattle.

The Route

0.0 Marble Mountain Sno-Park
0.6 Trail junction; cross to north
1.0 Junction with June Lake Trail 216-B; climb south
2.4 June Lake

The well-marked trails and roads around the south side of Mount St. Helens are great for cross-country skiers whose children want to try their own adventures on skinny skis or yearn to be pinheads like Mom and Dad.

The Pine Marten Trail—one of several that lead from the Sno-Park to June Lake—is a good place to start. Begin at the northeast end of the Sno-Park on the Pine Marten Trail, marked 245-E, and climb gently for about a half mile to a crossing with a spur road off Forest Road 83.

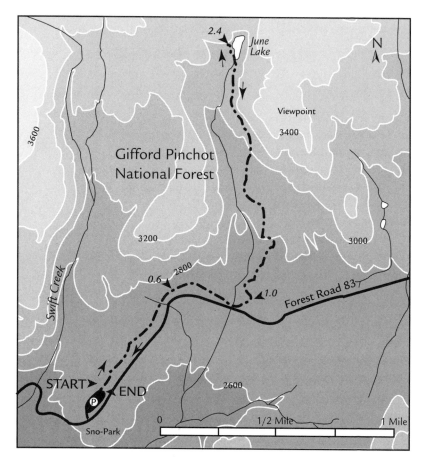

Continue above FR 83, turning to the east to a junction in another half mile with June Lake Trail 216-B. Turn north here and climb along the snow-covered creek draining June Lake for 1.4 miles to the lake.

Those looking for downhill adventure might find it on the open slope and ridge just west of the lake. This hill offers about 200 vertical feet.

29 Marble Mountain

❄

Distance:	12.0 miles
Base elevation:	2,600 feet
Elevation gain:	1,500 feet
Trail time:	7 hours
Trail type:	Forest road
Skill level:	Novice
Avalanche potential:	Low
Traction advisory:	Waxable, waxless
Maps:	Green Trails 364; USGS Mount Mitchell (7.5' series)

Getting There

From I-5 at Woodland, about 115 miles south of Tacoma, take exit 21 and follow State Route 503 east through Cougar to Forest Road 83. Follow FR 83 to the Marble Mountain Sno-Park (designated Cougar Sno-Park on the 1997–98 Washington Cross Country Ski Sno-Park pamphlet). Allow about three and a half hours travel time from Seattle.

The Route

0.0   Marble Mountain Sno-Park
1.3   Junction with Forest Road 120; keep left
4.0   Junction with Forest Road 480; switchback left
6.0   Marble Mountain summit

Forest Road 8312, which first descends, then climbs to the southeast to the summit of 4,100-foot Marble Mountain, is a good trip for cross-country skiing families whose children are too young to ski and need hauling on a sled. It's open and offers great views when the winter days are clear.

From the Sno-Park, walk south across FR 83 about 50 yards to the beginning of FR 8312. Once on FR 8312, don skis and follow it as it drops slightly to cross tributaries to Swift Creek.

Just beyond, the road arcs to the south and begins to climb past a junction with FR 120. Continue climbing south on FR 8312 around a valley, turning

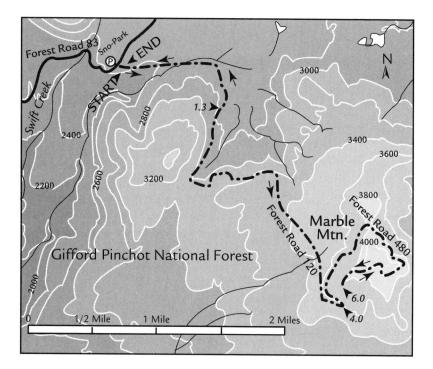

east at its head for about a half mile. The road then curves south again before switching back at 4.0 miles—the junction with FR 480—and winding around Marble Mountain to its summit.

It is possible to climb the slopes of Marble Mountain from the north side—or to descend that way—cutting about a mile off the road tour.

30 Mount St. Helens

❄❄❄❄½

Distance:	8.0 miles
Base elevation:	2,600 feet
Elevation gain:	5,700 feet
Trail time:	9 hours
Trail type:	Summer trail, backcountry
Skill level:	Advanced
Avalanche potential:	Considerable
Traction advisory:	Skins
Maps:	Green Trails 364S; USGS Mount St. Helens (7.5' series)

A skier crosses Swift Creek at Mount St. Helens.

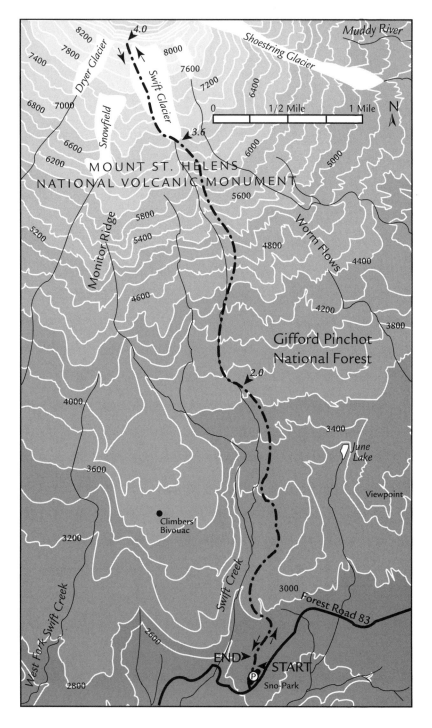

8200
7800
7400
8000
7600
7200
Muddy River
Shoestring Glacier
Dryer Glacier
4.0
Swift Glacier
6800
7000
6400
6000
5000
Snowfield
6600
6200
3.6
MOUNT ST. HELENS
NATIONAL VOLCANIC MONUMENT
5600
0   1/2 Mile   1 Mile
N
Worm Flows
4800
5800
Monitor Ridge
5400
4400
5200
4600
4200
Gifford Pinchot
National Forest
3800
4000
2.0
3400
June
Lake
Viewpoint
3600
Climbers'
Bivouac
3200
Swift Creek
3000
Forest Road 83
West Fork Swift Creek
2600
END
START
P
Sno-Park
2800

Getting There

From I-5 at Woodland, about 115 miles south of Tacoma, take exit 21 and follow State Route 503 east through Cougar to Forest Road 83. Follow FR 83 to the Marble Mountain Sno-Park (designated Cougar Sno-Park on the 1997–98 Washington Cross Country Ski Sno-Park pamphlet). Allow about three and a half hours travel time from Seattle.

In the winter, until May 15, you must issue yourself a $15 permit (1997–98) if you intend to climb above 4,800 feet. These are available at a registration box at Jack's Restaurant and Store, 5 miles west of Cougar on SR 503.

The Route

0.0   Marble Mountain Sno-Park
2.0   Junction with Trail 216; climb north
3.6   Swift Glacier
4.0   Crater rim

The winter route up Mount St. Helens provides downhillers with all the thrills—and all the climbing—they can handle in one day. You'll be using skins, snowshoes, or kicking steps up more than a vertical mile of winter snow that is often windblown and hard packed.

There are days in midwinter when you'll hit the perfect combination of snow and sunshine that makes this hill as close to heaven as you'll find. If you wait until late spring, you can start another 1,200 feet higher and stand a better chance of getting good corn snow.

Starting from the Sno-Park, climb Trail 244 along the eastern bank of Swift Creek to its junction with Trail 216 at about 3,700 feet. From here, climb to the north to gain a ridge crest at about 4,400 feet, just west of the Worm Flows.

Climb up the crest of the ridge, aiming for the smooth cup of the Swift Glacier to the northwest. You should gain the snowclad glacier at its snout, around 6,600 feet, and climb in an ascending traverse to the west side of the glacier at around 8,000 feet.

The crest of the rim, 8,365 feet, is a third of a mile west from the Swift Glacier—but the view doesn't get significantly better. If you've gotten an early start, you may have time to enjoy it before the long ride home.

Mount Adams

Towering 12,276 feet into the stratosphere, Mount Adams would seem to be an ideal winter playground—and indeed it is for those who have the time to travel long distances on forest roads or own a snowmobile that can whisk them to the slopes. The rest of us must wait until the roads open in the spring to get a really good ride on the mountain itself. (See "Extending the Season" at the end of this book.)

There are some excellent high tours around the mountain, however, on typically better snow than you'll find in most of the Cascades. The two tours here are recommended for that reason.

31 MOUNT ADAMS
Peterson Ridge
❄❄

Distance:	11.0 miles
Base elevation:	2,700 feet
Elevation gain:	1,200 feet
Trail time:	6 hours
Trail type:	Forest road
Skill level:	Intermediate
Avalanche potential:	Low
Traction advisory:	Skins, waxable
Maps:	Green Trails 398; USGS Quigley Butte (7.5' series)

Getting There

From Seattle, take I-5 south to Portland, Oregon. Then head east on I-84 for 69 miles to Hood River, where you take the toll bridge to Bingen and follow State Route 14 west to SR 141. Turn north on SR 141 and follow it about 22 miles to the town of Trout Lake and then another 9 miles to the end of the plowed road at the Atkisson Sno-Park. Allow about 5 hours travel time from Seattle.

The Route

0.0 Atkisson Sno-Park
1.0 Junction with Forest Road 2420; turn right
3.6 Junction with Forest Road N67; turn right
4.5 Peterson Ridge; turn left
5.5 Turnaround

This cross-country tour climbs gently west for about a mile along Forest Road 24 before a junction with FR 2420. At the junction, turn northeast and follow FR 2420 as it gently climbs and drops and climbs again around the west base of Peterson Ridge.

At about a mile from the junction, the way turns to the southeast. After climbing around a wide gully, it ascends more steeply to a junction with FR N67 at 3.6 miles. Switchback along this road to the southwest, climbing to the crest of Peterson Ridge at about 3,600 feet.

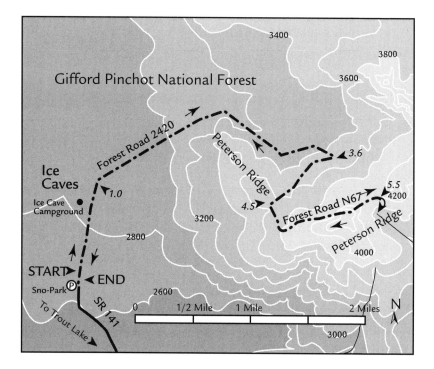

From this low point in a saddle on the ridge, turn first northeast, then east-northeast along a road to the crest of the ridge again, this time at about 3,900 feet.

32 MOUNT ADAMS
Aiken Lava Bed
❄ ½

Distance:	7.6 miles
Base elevation:	3,800 feet
Elevation gain:	1,100 feet
Trail time:	4 hours
Trail type:	Forest road, backcountry
Skill level:	Intermediate
Avalanche potential:	None
Traction advisory:	Waxable, waxless
Maps:	U.S. Forest Service, Mount Adams Ranger District; USGS Trout Lake (7.5' series)

Getting There

From Seattle, take I-5 south to Portland, Oregon. Then head east on I-84 for 69 miles to Hood River, where you take the toll bridge to Bingen and follow State Route 14 west to SR 141. Turn north on SR 141 and follow it about 22 miles to the town of Trout Lake. From Trout Lake, turn off SR 141 at the Mount Adams Recreation Area sign to the right. Follow this road for 9 miles, keeping right at three intersections. This road becomes Forest Road 82 to Pine Side Sno-Park and Smith Butte Sno-Park at 3,800 feet. If the road isn't plowed to Smith Butte Sno-Park, return to Pine Side and ski groomed loops there. Allow about 5 hours travel time from Seattle.

The Route

0.0 Smith Butte Sno-Park
1.0 Junction with Forest Road 60; turn left
1.3 Junction with Forest Road 71; turn right
2.5 Junction with Forest Road 150; turn right
3.5 Road ends
3.8 Aiken overlook

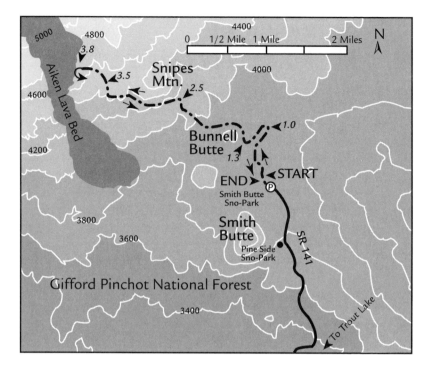

This tour up and down gently graded logging roads follows a route through forest and view-yielding clear-cuts to a 4,500-foot knoll overlooking the massive Aiken Lava Bed.

From the Sno-Park, ski north and northwest, gradually climbing on Forest Road 82 to a junction at 3,900 feet with FR 60. Turn left and southwest to the base of Bunnell Butte and take FR 71 around the base of this 4,100-foot lump. An old Forest Service map shows a gravel pit on the southwest side, where you may find unexplored (and untested) downhill opportunities.

At about 2.5 miles, you'll come to a junction with FR 150, which climbs to the right before switching back and climbing more moderately to end at about 4,500 feet. To continue, cross the creek gully and climb a broad slope to the northwest to the 4,582-foot knob above the 3-mile-long Aiken Lava Bed.

Blewett Pass

If you're going to see the sunshine anywhere in the Cascades on any given weekend, the Blewett Pass area is where you'll find it. This is one of the only north-south highway corridors in the Cascades. Sheltered by the front range, the pass hides from clouds sweeping in from the Pacific Ocean, clouds popped like puffy water balloons by the time they reach Blewett.

So the sun appears here more frequently, and you may think all those rain-bleached Puget Sounders are telemarking, but actually they are genuflecting to old Sol. Here, near the summit of 4,100-foot Blewett Pass, you'll find everything from flat meadow tours to a steep west-facing hill guaranteed to have you reaching for the ibuprofen at the end of the day.

A final, curious note: Blewett Pass lies in an area known as a geoetymological anomaly area, manifested by the strange things that happen to words as they pass by. "Blewett," for example, changed to "Swauk" for a couple of decades, then back to Blewett. And Tronsen Meadows and Campground became "Tronson Meadows" and "Tronson Campground" on the Green Trails map—despite the fact that "Tronsen Creek" on the same map remained unchanged. Nobody can explain it.

33 BLEWETT PASS
Tronsen Meadows
❄❄

Distance:	3.0 miles
Base elevation:	3,900 feet
Elevation gain:	700 feet
Trail time:	2 hours
Trail type:	Forest road, marked trail
Skill level:	Intermediate
Avalanche potential:	Low
Traction advisory:	Waxless
Maps:	Green Trails 210; USGS Swauk Pass (7.5' series)

Getting There

From Seattle, drive east on I-90 over Snoqualmie Pass to the easternmost Cle Elum exit, State Route 970, and follow the signs to Wenatchee. In 12 miles, SR 970 joins US Highway 97. Turn north here and follow US 97 to Blewett Pass, then about three-quarters of a mile farther to plowed parking areas at FR 7240 or, another half mile down the road, FR 7230. If these small areas are full, park at the Swauk Pass Sno-Park at the summit of the pass. Allow about one and a half hours travel time from Seattle.

The Route

0.0	Forest Road 7240 parking area
0.1	Gated forest road; turn left
1.0	Trail forks; keep left
1.7	Trail forks; downhillers turn left, tourers keep right
2.3	Forest Road 7245; turn left
2.7	Join Forest Road 7240
2.9	US Highway 97; turn left
3.0	Parking area

This route, which climbs around and circles Tronsen Meadows, is but one of many combinations of the marked—but mostly ungroomed—trails around the summit of Blewett Pass. Loops of up to 8.5 miles are possible. Mostly set for cross-country skiers with novice to advanced skills, the trails wind through stands of mature pine and selectively logged areas where midwinter snow cover allows opportunities for good tree-slalom snowriding.

Climb above the highway to the right, or southeast, for about 0.1 mile to a road that climbs to the left. Climb on the road for about a mile to a trail intersection. Stay to the left on the road.

Logging roads provide good forest trails around Tronsen Meadows.

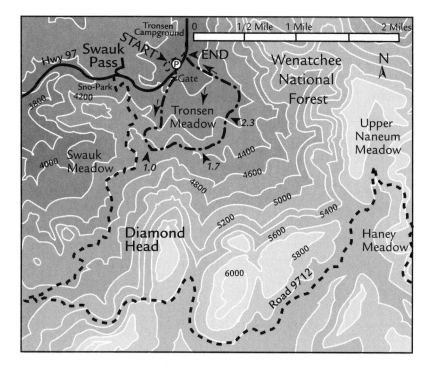

At about 1.5 miles, the road ends and the trail continues to a junction at 1.7 miles, about 4,600 feet. Those seeking a downhill rush can turn left on the marked trail and swing through the pines 600 vertical feet to Forest Road 7240 below.

The ski tour continues to contour another half mile to the upper reaches of FR 7245. Turn left here and ski down the road, joining FR 7240 in about a half mile. Ski FR 7240 back to US 97 and turn left above the highway to ski back to the parking area.

34 BLEWETT PASS
Forest Road 800
❄❄½

Distance:	6.0 miles
Base elevation:	4,100 feet
Elevation gain:	400 feet
Trail time:	3 hours
Trail type:	Forest road
Skill level:	Novice
Avalanche potential:	Low
Traction advisory:	Waxless
Maps:	Green Trails 210; USGS Swauk Pass (7.5' series)

The Wunderhund tests snow on Forest Road 800.

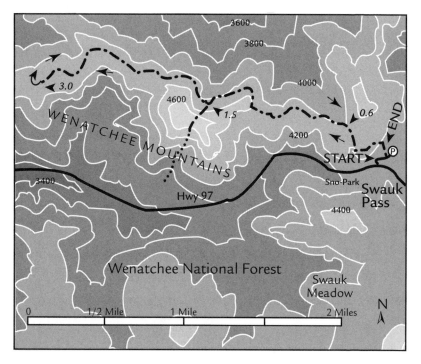

Getting There

From Seattle, drive east on I-90 over Snoqualmie Pass to the easternmost Cle Elum exit, State Route 970, and follow the signs to Wenatchee. In 12 miles, SR 970 joins US Highway 97. Turn north here and follow US 97 to Blewett Pass, then continue to the Swauk Pass Sno-Park at the summit of the pass and park on the north side of the Sno-Park. Allow about one and a half hours travel time from Seattle.

The Route

0.0 Swauk Pass Sno-Park
0.1 Road branches; stay left
0.6 Road branches; stay left
1.5 Peak 4745; thrill-seekers climb left
3.0 Road ends

Choose this easy tour if you've got youngsters who like cruising snow-covered roads or if you've got youngsters who would prefer to blast off through steep clear-cuts or forest glades. In other words, choose this tour if you've got youngsters in tow.

If you want downhill adventure, you can find it at any of several clear-cut areas or in open pine forests. You'll even find a steep south-facing meadow atop Peak 4745.

Begin by skiing up the gentle road from the parking lot to a flat knoll underneath splendid old pine trees at about 0.1 mile. Those who just can't wait for downhill thrills can ski or ride off the knoll to the east-southeast for about 300 vertical feet below US 97.

Otherwise, continue on the road to the left, swinging southwest for about half a mile to a branch in the road. Take the left branch onto Forest Road 800.

This road alternately climbs and drops along or under the north side of a ridge formed by the Wenatchee Mountains above Swauk and Scotty Creeks. Logged areas, especially on the north side, provide good downhill runs of up to 500 vertical feet.

And, thanks to the Cascade front range to the west, the mostly pine woods are more open than west-slope fir forests. Skilled telemarkers and boarders can find plenty of yo-yo opportunities.

At about 1.5 miles, the road curves gently down into a wide gully formed by a Scotty Creek tributary. Peak 4745 is south of this gully, and downhillers should climb to the summit for a 400-vertical-foot run down the open south-facing meadow.

Cross-country skiers can continue along the road for another 1.5 miles, to where a ridge-crest lunch spot offers good views down the Swauk Valley.

35 BLEWETT PASS
Haney Meadow

❄❄❄½

Distance:	9.0 to 16.0 miles
Base elevation:	4,100 feet
Elevation gain/loss:	1,800 feet/400 feet
Trail time:	6 to 8 hours
Trail type:	Forest road, marked trail
Skill level:	Intermediate
Avalanche potential:	Moderate
Traction advisory:	Skins, waxless
Maps:	Green Trails 210; USGS Swauk Pass (7.5' series)

Swauk Meadows Trail leads to the Haney Meadow route.

Getting There

From Seattle, drive east on I-90 over Snoqualmie Pass to the easternmost Cle Elum exit, State Route 970, and follow the signs to Wenatchee. In 12 miles, SR 970 joins US Highway 97. Turn north here and follow US 97 to Blewett Pass, then continue to the Swauk Pass Sno-Park at the summit of the pass and park in the Sno-Park's larger parking lot on the south side of US 97. This parking area is frequently filled with RVs and snowmobile rigs. If this is the case, try the parking areas just north of the pass or the Pipe Creek Sno-Park just south of the pass. Allow about one and a half hours travel time from Seattle.

The Route

0.0 Swauk Pass Sno-Park
0.6 Haney Meadow ski route; climb left
1.7 Trail junction; keep right
2.7 Trail junction; climb left
3.4 Forest Road 1209
4.5 Haney Meadow

There are two basic routes to Haney Meadow, a splendid alpine playland for both snowmobilers and skiers complete with a log cabin and steep, gladed runs for telemark travelers. The route described here is for cross-country skiers with intermediate skills.

Novice skiers will likely have more fun skiing up Forest Roads 9716 and 9712, routes shared with—and nicely packed down by—snowmobile riders. Skiers wishing to set their own track on this road can usually do so by stepping off the road uphill or downhill a few feet. These roads add another 7 miles to the round trip to Haney Meadow.

For the steeper, shorter ski trail, ski up FR 9716 for about 0.6 mile to the Haney Meadow Trail on the left. This is a well-marked trail that climbs through pine forest and selectively logged areas that offer good downhill possibilities for snowriders who enjoy expending their energy on yo-yo hills.

At about 4,800 feet and 1.7 miles, the trail branches, with the left fork dropping back to FR 7240 and the north side of Blewett Pass. Continue climbing to the right, around the steep east face of Diamond Head. Two avalanche chutes must be crossed along this section of trail.

In another mile and 700 feet up, you'll find another trail junction. To the right, you can climb in a fifth of a mile through a saddle to FR 9712. The left

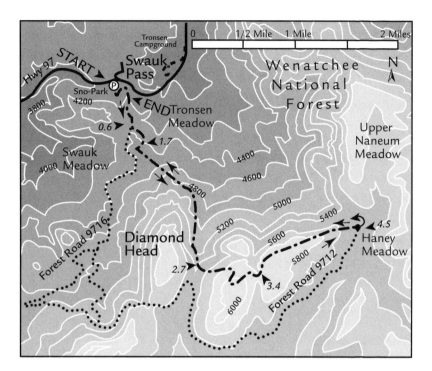

fork leads to the high point of your climb, a round, 5,900-foot peak with downhill possibilities to FR 9712 below, to the south.

To reach Haney Meadow, ski across the summit of this peak to FR 1209, at 3.4 miles. This road drops gently in 1.1 miles to 5,500-foot Haney Meadow.

For an excellent, steep north-facing run of about 600 vertical feet, ski southwest on FR 9712 for about 2 miles to a junction with the Table Mountain Road and follow FR 9712 down to the steep bowl just south of Diamond Head. (This area is outlined in Route 36, Diamond Head.)

36 BLEWETT PASS
Diamond Head
❄❄❄❄

Distance:	4.0 miles
Base elevation:	4,100 feet
Elevation gain:	1,800 feet
Trail time:	5 hours
Trail type:	Forest road, backcountry
Skill level:	Advanced
Avalanche potential:	Moderate
Traction advisory:	Skins, waxless
Maps:	Green Trails 210; USGS Swauk Pass (7.5' series)

Diamond Head offers open slopes close to the Blewett Pass Highway.

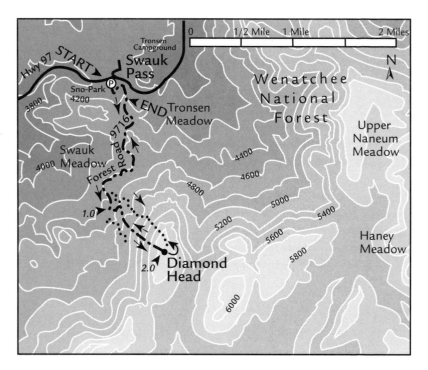

Getting There

From Seattle, drive east on I-90 over Snoqualmie Pass to the easternmost Cle Elum exit, State Route 970, and follow the signs to Wenatchee. In 12 miles, SR 970 joins US Highway 97. Turn north here and follow US 97 to Blewett Pass, then continue to the Swauk Pass Sno-Park at the summit of the pass and park in the Sno-Park's larger parking lot on the south side of US 97. This parking area is frequently filled with RVs and snowmobile rigs. If this is the case, try the parking areas just north of the pass or the Pipe Creek Sno-Park just south of the pass. Allow about one and a half hours travel time from Seattle.

The Route

0.0 Swauk Pass Sno-Park
1.0 Road junction; climb left
2.0 Diamond Head summit

The steep, open west face of Diamond Head is the best downhill slope convenient to the Blewett Pass area, easily the top choice here for backcountry boarders. It's probably best in the early spring, when the sun has had a chance to turn the frequently wind-scoured slopes to corn.

But there will be midwinter days when the sun shines and there's a cold blanket of powder on those slopes. On such a day, Diamond Head sparkles.

From the parking lot, follow Forest Road 9716 as it climbs gently south. If you wish to avoid snowmobiles, stay uphill or downhill of the road, or follow the marked ski trail that turns off the road at about a fifth of a mile.

Follow the road for about 2.0 miles, until it crosses directly under the west face of Diamond Head at about 4,500 feet. A spur road branches left and switches back right at this point and you may climb on it or switchback southeast to the 5,915-foot summit. Distance will vary depending upon your aerobic conditioning and how well your climbing skins work.

Rest at the summit. Admire the great view. Pick your line. Hoo-haw.

Do not, under any circumstances, make the mistake your humble correspondent did in initially scouting this route. Seeing that FR 141 appeared to climb directly from the Pipe Creek Sno-Park to the base of Diamond Head, he set off on it for what promised to be a splendid day. Unfortunately, the road ended somewhat short of the goal in an undiscovered section of the Grand Canyon, where a tree well temporarily swallowed Tar, the wunderhund, a miniature poodle who thinks he can ski.

Salmon La Sac

Although the mountains around the Salmon La Sac area offer excellent skiing in the spring, after the roads open, access is a problem in winter. The road is plowed to Salmon La Sac, although in times of major storms, it may be the last road that plows get to.

Though several hills are accessible here, along with a number of good tours along the Cle Elum River or up Thorp Creek, the Howson Creek Trail might be the best choice for downhill adventure. If you enjoy late spring or early summer, revisit the area later to try Mount Daniel.

The snow in the Salmon La Sac area is generally lighter than the stuff that falls on the west side of the Cascades. You'll also stand a better chance of seeing that warm, golden orb Puget Sounders have come to know only fleetingly.

37 | SALMON LA SAC
Howson Creek
❊❊❊

Distance: 6.0 miles
Base elevation: 2,300 feet
Elevation gain: 1,600 feet
Trail time: 3.5 hours
Trail type: Forest road
Skill level: Intermediate
Avalanche potential: Low
Traction advisory: Skins, waxless
Maps: Green Trails 208; USGS Cle Elum Lake (7.5' series)

Getting There

From Seattle, drive east on I-90 to the Cle Elum exit 80. Follow State Route 903 to Roslyn and take the Salmon La Sac Road north past Cle Elum Lake. Drive a fifth of a mile north of the Red Mountain Campground to a small plowed pullout on the east side of the road. This is the start of Forest Road 128, which climbs Sasse Ridge to the east. If the pullout is not plowed, or there is no room, you should be able to find parking 1 mile north at the junction of Cooper River Road and Salmon La Sac Road. Allow about one and a half hours travel time from Seattle.

The Route

0.0 Parking area at Forest Road 128
0.3 First switchback
1.3 Second switchback
2.3 Clear-cut
3.0 Top of clear-cut

This route climbs the ridge between Howson Creek and Little Salmon La Sac to the top of a clear-cut at about 3,900 feet. Those willing to climb for about 2 miles and 800 feet will be rewarded with 800 vertical feet of wide-open snowriding.

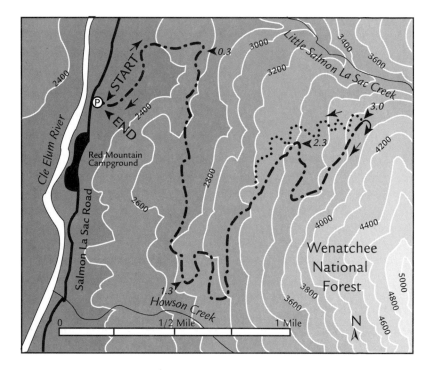

Begin by climbing gently to the north for about 0.3 mile to a wide switch-back. This part of the route, as well as the next mile, would make a good tour for the entire family. After switching back, the road climbs to the south for about a mile. This section is initially steep, but flattens out on a bench to climb more gently to about 2,800 feet.

Follow the road for three more short switchbacks to the base of a clear-cut at about 3,100 feet and climb to the top of the clear-cut to the northeast. On the way up, admire the view and try to make an assessment of the amount of logging slash you'll have to avoid on the way down. In years of low snow, this could be a real hazard.

Snoqualmie Pass/I-90

Here, on mountains a scant one hour away for most Seattle-area riders and skiers, you'll find long cross-country tours along the flats, and stump slaloms in steep clear-cuts. Expect company on most of these routes, especially on weekends—but know, too, that you'll be able to find spots where your only company will be gray jays begging for a handout.

Because Snoqualmie Pass is the lowest of the Cascade passes, it is the most likely to receive precipitation that is not in the light, crystalline form. We are talking here about the "R" word, which should never be spoken out loud.

If you plan winter snow play here, the best advice is to be prepared for any kind of weather. Snoqualmie is an excellent destination choice to discover whether your waterproof-breathable parka really works. Look at it this way: If it weren't for days when such tests are possible, you wouldn't appreciate the great days at Snoqualmie—days that indeed exist.

38 Mount Catherine

❄❄½

Distance:	6.0 miles
Base elevation:	2,500 feet
Elevation gain:	1,300 feet
Trail time:	4 hours
Trail type:	Forest road, backcountry
Skill level:	Intermediate
Avalanche potential:	Low
Traction advisory:	Waxable
Maps:	Green Trails 207; USGS Snoqualmie Pass, Lost Lake (7.5' series)

Getting There

From Seattle, drive east on I-90 over Snoqualmie Pass to the Hyak exit 54. Turn left and follow Forest Road 2219 to the Keechelus Sno-Park, 1.5 miles south of the exit at the Keechelus boat launch. Allow about one hour travel time from Seattle.

The Route

0.0 Keechelus Sno-Park
0.2 Forest Road 9070
1.6 First switchback
2.0 Switchback
3.0 Windy Pass

The first part of this route is along a sometimes-groomed track and part of a "shared corridor." It is shared by the commercial nordic operation at Snoqualmie ski area and the public. You'll also cross the Iron Horse Trail, a groomed cross-country ski trail in the winter that provides an 8-mile run along the quiet west shore of Keechelus Lake.

Climb from the Sno-Park across the Iron Horse Trail to Forest Road 9070, which descends to cross Mill Creek before climbing to the west-southwest into Cold Creek basin. The road climbs gently for about a mile after entering the basin to an old clear-cut, where it switches back at about 3,000 feet.

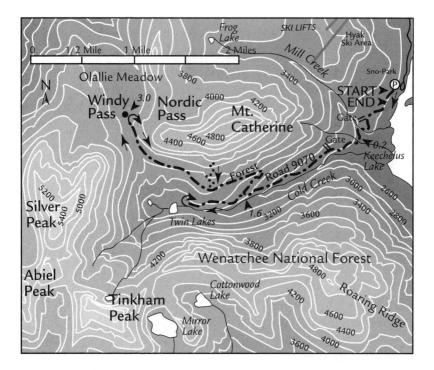

Cross-country skiers looking for a spot of solitude might find it by continuing to climb up the Cold Creek drainage for about three-quarters of a mile to Twin Lakes basin. Other skiers must turn east and follow the road as it climbs up the lower slopes of Mount Catherine.

The road switches back again after about half a mile and 3,200 feet to climb west for another mile toward Windy Pass, where the shared trail ends. Beyond this point, the commercial operation takes over, and if you want to ski farther without paying, stay off the prepared and groomed track.

You'll find downhill thrills by skiing or riding the steep south face of Mount Catherine through old clear-cuts or by cutting switchbacks on the road.

39 SNOQUALMIE PASS/I-90
Silver Peak
❄❄❄❄

Distance:	8.0 miles
Base elevation:	2,500 feet
Elevation gain:	3,100 feet
Trail time:	7.5 hours
Trail type:	Forest road, backcountry
Skill level:	Advanced
Avalanche potential:	Considerable
Traction advisory:	Skins, waxable
Maps:	Green Trails 207; USGS Snoqualmie Pass, Lost Lake (7.5' series)

Getting There

From Seattle, drive east on I-90 over Snoqualmie Pass to the Hyak exit 54. Turn left and follow Forest Road 2219 to the Keechelus Sno-Park, 1.5 miles south of the exit, at the Keechelus boat launch. Allow about one hour travel time from Seattle.

The Route

0.0 Keechelus Sno-Park
3.0 Windy Pass
4.0 Silver Peak

Stretching its white mantle 5,605 feet into the sky, Silver Peak has long been a popular destination for backcountry ski mountaineers around Snoqualmie Pass. It provides steep downhill runs of almost 1,800 vertical feet along a north-facing ridge, perhaps the best backcountry snowriding on naturally open slopes that Snoqualmie has to offer.

Begin by following the common corridor, Forest Road 9070, to Windy Pass. Avoid skiing any of the commercially groomed trails beyond Windy Pass. From the pass, ski west up a wide, flat ridge just north of the snow-covered creek draining the bowl underneath Silver Peak.

Turn south along the ridge at about 4,000 feet, climbing along the ridge and avoiding cornices to the west. The ridge becomes increasingly steeper

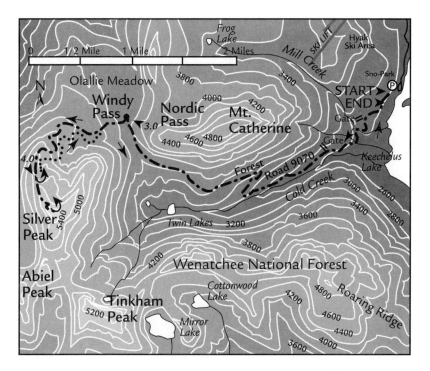

and sharper at about 4,800 feet, and snowriders with little mountaineering experience may want to begin their descent here.

Extremists may continue up the ridge, perhaps kicking steps for the final hundred feet. Best route off the summit is to retrace the climb up.

40 SNOQUALMIE PASS/I-90
Kendall Peak
❄❄❄½

Distance:	4.0 miles
Base elevation:	2,900 feet
Elevation gain:	2,300 feet
Trail time:	4 hours
Trail type:	Backcountry
Skill level:	Intermediate
Avalanche potential:	Moderate
Traction advisory:	Skins, waxable
Maps:	Green Trails 207; USGS Snoqualmie Pass (7.5' series)

Stump slalom, Kendall Ridge.

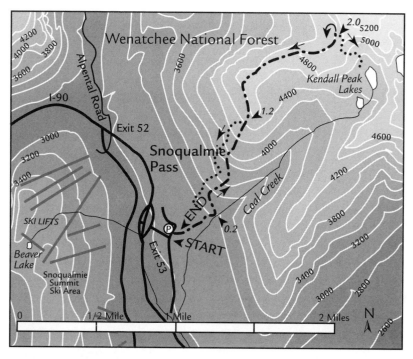

Getting There

From Seattle, drive east on I-90 over Snoqualmie Pass to exit 53. Turn left and park on the side of the road. Signs direct skiers to park on opposite sides of the road on alternating days. Allow about one hour travel time from Seattle.

The Route

0.0 Road parking
0.2 Clear-cut
1.2 Kendall Ridge
2.0 Turnaround point

The clear-cut west slopes below Kendall Peak provide some of the most convenient backcountry downhill that can be found at Snoqualmie Pass. If you arrive on a day following a major storm, you'll probably have company riding here. To put things back into perspective, look west across I-90 to the hordes at the ski area.

From the road, climb due east between private ski cabins in the forest just north of the spot where the road turns south. You'll climb through woods for about 0.2 mile, emerging at the lower end of a clear-cut just above the spot where Coal Creek turns south.

Stay above Coal Creek on the north side, switching back along the tree line to about 3,600 feet, then aim for a bald knoll on the ridge in front of you. This south-facing ridge may be rocky at the knoll in years of low snow.

Climb to the knoll, cresting the ridge at about 4,400 feet, and climb north about 200 vertical feet before turning east again to follow the ridge crest to about 5,200 feet. This makes a good lunch spot and turnaround point.

From here, you can swoop directly southeast into the bowl below Kendall Lakes for a run of about 800 vertical feet, or follow your tracks down the ridge to the knoll. You can drop off the knoll for about 1,200 vertical feet into Coal Creek, aiming for the spot where you emerged from the forest.

41 | SNOQUALMIE PASS/I-90
Mount Margaret
✻✻✻

Distance:	12.0 miles
Base elevation:	2,500 feet
Elevation gain:	2,700 feet
Trail time:	6 hours
Trail type:	Logging road, backcountry
Skill level:	Intermediate
Avalanche potential:	Moderate
Traction advisory:	Skins, waxless
Maps:	Green Trails 207; USGS Stampede Pass (7.5' series)

Getting There

From Seattle, drive east on I-90 over Snoqualmie Pass to the Hyak exit 54. Turn left and follow the signs to the Gold Creek Sno-Park. Park as far south along the road as you can. Allow about one hour travel time from Seattle.

The Route

0.0 Gold Creek Sno-Park
1.9 Wolfe Creek; road switches back
3.4 Road forks; climb left
3.9 Road forks; climb left
6.0 Margaret saddle

The reward for this long climb is a good downhill return through clear-cuts for almost 2,000 vertical feet. The view from the top isn't bad either, since it includes that big mountain to the south where you'll find wide-open snowriding created by nature, not loggers. That would be Mount Rainier.

But Mount Margaret is a good choice if you catch good weather and start early enough to carve a few figure 8s in the slopes. Begin by skiing along the old highway for 2 miles, paralleling I-90 and the traffic noise. (It helps to remember during these trying times that, were it not for that noisy road next to you, you would not be here.)

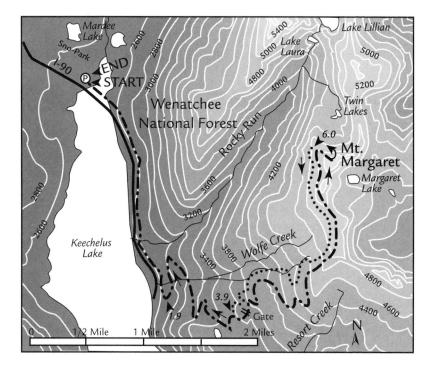

At about 1.9 miles, you'll cross Wolfe Creek and switchback to begin climbing steeply. You'll gain 600 feet, switching back four times before the road forks at about 3,300 feet. Climb to the left and switchback twice before the road forks again, at 3.9 miles.

Turn left, up the hill past a gate, and continue climbing steeply through clear-cuts, keeping the upper reaches of Wolfe Creek on your left and the sharp ridge climbing north to Mount Margaret on your right. At about 4,600 feet, the route begins an ascending traverse to the north, toward the low point in the ridge above.

Climb to this point at 5,200 feet. Margaret Lake lies in the bowl to the northeast; Mount Margaret is a half mile north. Cornices sometimes form along the crest of this ridge.

Return along the way you climbed, slicing all those switchbacks through the clear-cut areas to ribbons.

42 SNOQUALMIE PASS/I-90
Keechelus Ridge
❋❋❋

Distance:	8.4 miles
Base elevation:	2,500 feet
Elevation gain:	2,600 feet
Trail time:	4 hours
Trail type:	Forest road
Skill level:	Intermediate
Avalanche potential:	Moderate
Traction advisory:	Skins, waxless
Maps:	Green Trails 207; USGS Stampede Pass (7.5' series)

Keechelus Lake lies at the base of Keechelus Ridge, left, and Mt. Catherine, right.

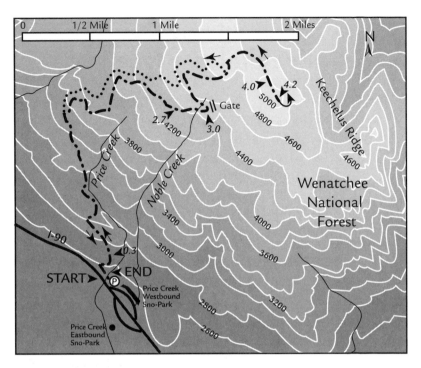

Getting There

From Seattle, drive east on I-90 over Snoqualmie Pass to the Stampede Pass exit 62. Turn left across the freeway and take I-90 west for a mile to the Price Creek Sno-Park. Allow a little more than an hour travel time from Seattle.

The Route

- **0.0** Price Creek Sno-Park
- **0.3** Forest Road 4832; cross to Forest Road 124
- **2.7** Forest Road 4934; continue to climb
- **3.0** Road forks; climb left
- **4.0** Ridge crest
- **4.2** Peak 5,154

Here's yet more evidence that without the invention of the chain saw, back-country snowriding around Snoqualmie Pass wouldn't be nearly so much fun. Climb this hill for more than 2,000 vertical feet of clear-cut skiing.

This hill is at its best when snow depths reach their maximum around mid-March. With such a low starting elevation, you'll need all the white stuff you can get to cover the stumps and slash.

Begin at the north end of the Sno-Park area and climb to and cross Forest Road 4832, a groomed snowmobile road. You'll find FR 124 just across the road, climbing steeply to the north.

Climb up this road and cross another snowmobile route, FR 4934, at about 4,300 feet. Continue climbing to a fork in the road about a third of a mile past the crossing. Take the left fork and climb to a saddle between the 4,960-foot hill on your left and the 5,154-foot hill on your right. Ascend the ridge to the south to the summit of Peak 5,154.

The top makes an excellent spot for lunch and surveying the countryside in good weather. Mount Rainier stretches across the horizon to the south, while Mount Stuart is that big cloud-gouger to the east.

43 Amabilis Mountain
❄❄❄

Distance:	9.4 miles
Base elevation:	2,200 feet
Elevation gain:	2,300 feet
Trail time:	5 hours
Trail type:	Forest road
Skill level:	Intermediate
Avalanche potential:	Low
Traction advisory:	Skins, waxless
Maps:	Green Trails 207; USGS Stampede Pass (7.5' series)

Getting There

From Seattle, drive east on I-90 over Snoqualmie Pass to the Cabin Creek exit 63. Park in the Cabin Creek Sno-Park. You'll need a Sno-Park permit and, on crowded days, perhaps even a Sherman tank to find a spot. Be sure to check the lower lot. Allow a little more than an hour travel time from Seattle.

The Route

- **0.0** Cabin Creek Sno-Park
- **0.5** Forest Road 4822; climb right
- **2.5** Road forks; switchback left
- **3.5** Switchback
- **4.7** Summit

The wide-open clear-cuts that made Amabilis Mountain a great backcountry downhill destination have grown up some in the past two decades, so snowriding isn't the hoo-haw it used to be. Nevertheless, you should find enough open spots for a good downhill run or two and, when conditions permit, a fine powder chute off the north side.

Begin by skiing past the groomed lanes of a ski racing club and climb right on Forest Road 4822 at 0.5 mile. This road switches back several times and climbs steeply up the west-facing slope of the flat-topped Amabilis Mountain, just above.

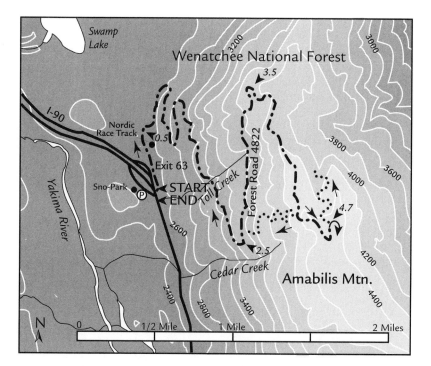

Continue climbing to about 3,400 feet, 2.5 miles, where the road branches. Go left. (The branch to the right loops across the top of the mountain, but the left branch climbs more directly to the top.)

You'll climb about another mile to a broad switchback at about 3,800 feet and climb a little over another mile along the open ridge top to the summit at about 4,560 feet. The ridge is exposed to frequent winds that may pack the west-facing slopes. When conditions permit, the gully to the north could offer the best riding for boarders patient enough to climb this far.

You can descend along the road or drop directly to the west where clear-cuts allow, intersecting the road at 3,400 feet. Alder and a growing cash crop of evergreens may halt downhill thrills at this point in any but the best snow years.

Stevens Pass

This is the closest place to the big city where you'll have your best chance of finding light snow. Steep, excellent north- and east-facing slopes collect white stuff that settles softly in the lee of the Cascade front range.

For convenience to civilization and access to the hills, it's tough to find a better spot for backcountry downhill adventures. If there is a single caution, it would be that the Stevens area is historically more prone to massive, destructive avalanches such as the one that wiped out part of Yodelin ski village in 1971. As always, if there's any doubt about avalanche risk, err on the side of caution. The slopes of Stevens Pass will be there for at least another day.

44 STEVENS PASS
Skyline Bowl
❄❄❄½

Distance:	2.0 to 4.0 miles
Base elevation:	4,050 feet
Elevation gain:	1,150 feet
Trail time:	2 to 5 hours
Trail type:	Backcountry, summer trail
Skill level:	Intermediate
Avalanche potential:	Considerable
Traction advisory:	Skins, waxless
Maps:	Green Trails 144; USGS Stevens Pass, Labyrinth Mountain (7.5' series)

The Skyline Bowl route is well marked and sometimes packed by snow-machines.

Getting There

From Seattle, follow I-5 north to US Highway 2, exit 194, and take US 2 east to Monroe. (Alternatively, take I-405 and State Route 522 to US 2 at Monroe.) From Monroe, follow US 2 to Stevens Pass. Allow about two hours for the drive from Seattle, and longer if you stop to put on chains. Park in the area on the north side of the pass, across the highway from the Stevens Pass ski area.

The Route

0.0 Parking lot
1.0 Skyline Lake
1.2 Skyline Ridge
2.0 Tye Saddle

For the better part of a half century, Skyline Ridge has welcomed snowriders who take their cold fun on the wild side. The slopes just above Skyline Lake have taught many folks the foibles of the telemark (that's technical jargon: a foible is the noise pinheads make just before they eat large quantities of snow). Before there were lifts across the road, skiers with bear-trap cable bindings and real seal skins climbed to Skyline Lake. Today their grandchildren tote single, wide snowriding devices that remind their grandparents of another nearly obsolete contraption, the ironing board.

From the parking lot, climb north past the utility station and private ski lodges through old trees to open slopes at about 4,400 feet. Switchback up the crest of the ridge another 400 feet, where the ridge widens and flattens to the northwest.

Turn northwest and climb about 300 feet into the bowl of Skyline Lake. Intermediate skiers and riders will find good slopes with about 200 feet of vertical for practice around the lake.

For greater rip, climb northwest to the 5,200-foot saddle west-northwest of Skyline Lake. Across the ridge, you'll find a vast bowl and more than 1,200 feet of vertical snowriding to the northeast. These slopes hide their powder from the sun in the winter and surprise backcountry skiers who have climbed to them via the open, south-facing Skyline Ridge, which is frequently wind-scoured hard-pack.

To reach the open slopes to the northwest, stay on the crest of the ridge as high as possible and traverse toward a flat saddle above Tye Lake. The 5,476-foot peak to the north of the saddle was named by a person with a very accurate altimeter: Point 5476. There's a steep, open run into the bowl from this point.

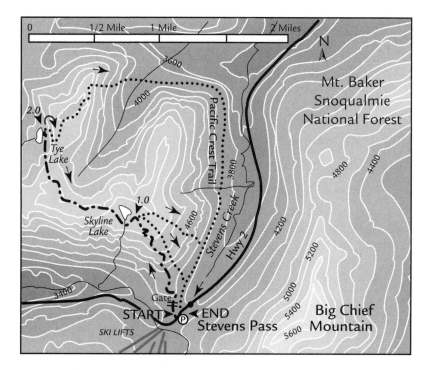

When good things come to an end—or when the thighs turn to quivering Jell-O, whichever comes first—there are two ways out of Skyline Bowl. The first involves tracking up all those fine figure 8s you've made and retracing your route uphill.

For the second, make one last run to the bottom of the bowl at about 3,800 feet, where the Pacific Crest Trail crosses the tributary to Nason Creek. Follow the trail to the right, or east, as it contours around Skyline Ridge and turns south to climb back to the parking lot.

This second route crosses several large avalanche chutes. Remember that if you choose to return via the second route, you'll be climbing at the end of the day, when you are least likely to want to practice avalanche swimming techniques.

45 STEVENS PASS
Valhalla Bowl
❄❄❄½

Distance:	7.0 miles
Elevation gain:	1,900 feet
Base elevation:	3,200 feet
Trail time:	4.5 hours
Trail type:	Forest road, backcountry
Skill level:	Intermediate
Avalanche potential:	Considerable
Traction advisory:	Skins, waxable, waxless
Maps:	Green Trails 144; USGS Stevens Pass, Labyrinth Mountain (7.5' series)

Getting There

From Seattle, follow I-5 north to US Highway 2, exit 194, and take US 2 east to Monroe. (Alternatively, take I-405 and State Route 522 to US 2 at Monroe.) From Monroe, follow US 2 east past Stevens Pass for 4 miles to the plowed area just east of Smith Brook Road (Forest Road 6700). Skiers from the west must drive 4.8 miles past Smith Brook Road, make a U-turn at Mill Creek, and drive back to the parking area. Park and ski or walk 100 yards east to Smith Brook Road. Allow about two hours for the drive from Seattle, and longer if you stop to put on chains.

The Route

0.0	Parking lot
0.7	First switchback
2.5	Road switches back; climb southwest
3.5	Valhalla Saddle

I might choose this vast powder stash for my home if I were a Norse god, or maybe if I won the lottery. You can't ask much more for a tour: The first half provides an excellent winter road ski for the family; the second, about 1,000 vertical feet of open and forested slopes.

Begin by climbing Smith Brook Road, gentle enough for waxable and waxless skis. The road parallels the creek for about 0.7 mile, then switches back

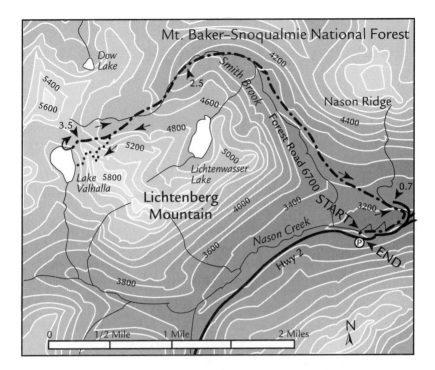

at about 3,300 feet. In another quarter mile, it turns back to the northwest and curves southwest to contour above Smith Brook.

The road climbs northwest above the creek to about 4,000 feet and 2.5 miles from the parking area. At this point, the road switches back, eventually climbing to a pass on Nason Ridge. This is a good turnaround point for those who enjoy touring over turning.

To continue, leave the road at the switchback and continue climbing southwest toward the lowest point between Lichtenberg Mountain, to the south, and Mount McCausland on the north.

This 5,100-foot-high saddle is your turnaround spot, unless the 200-foot slope down to Lake Valhalla to the southwest tempts you. Remember, however, that you must climb up what you ride down.

If you pass up the diversion to Lake Valhalla, pick your line back down to the road during lunch and a rest. For a run not interrupted by the flat meadow about 300 feet below and northeast of the saddle, traverse at about the 5,000-foot level to the northeast. About eight feet beneath you lies the Pacific Crest Trail.

46 | STEVENS PASS
Nason Saddle
❄❄❄½

Distance:	7.5 miles
Base elevation:	3,200 feet
Elevation gain:	1,400 feet
Trail time:	4 hours
Trail type:	Forest road, backcountry
Skill level:	Intermediate
Avalanche potential:	Considerable
Traction advisory:	Skins, waxless
Maps:	Green Trails 144; USGS Stevens Pass, Labyrinth Mountain (7.5' series)

Getting There

From Seattle, follow I-5 north to US Highway 2, exit 194, and take US 2 east to Monroe. (Alternatively, take I-405 and State Route 522 to US 2 at Monroe.) From Monroe, follow US 2 east past Stevens Pass for 4 miles to the plowed area just east of Smith Brook Road (Forest Road 6700). Skiers from the west must drive 4.8 miles past Smith Brook Road, make a U-turn at Mill Creek, and drive back to the parking area. Park and ski or walk 100 yards east to Smith Brook Road. Allow about two hours for the drive from Seattle, and longer if you stop to put on chains.

The Route

0.0 Parking area
0.7 First switchback
2.5 Road switches back
3.7 Nason Saddle

The slopes to the northeast of Nason Ridge offer another chance at drier snow that lingers when the stuff facing the winter sunset has long since popped into corn. You'll find runs of about 600 vertical feet from the saddle.

Climb up Smith Brook Road, which switches back at 0.7 mile, then back again, before climbing to another switchback at 2.5 miles. Up to this point, the route is a good one for cross-country touring.

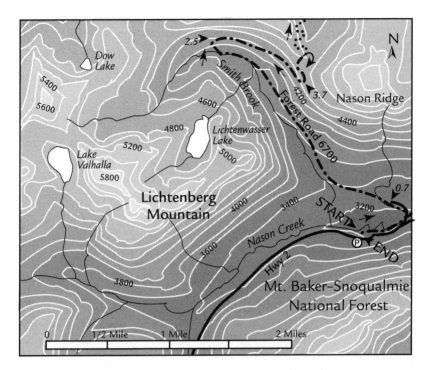

Snowriders headed for Valhalla Bowl (Route 45) would continue southwest at this switchback. But for Nason Saddle, follow the road back to the east as it climbs to the 4,600-foot saddle at the base of Nason Ridge. (As an alternative, skiers may climb the steep hill just west of the first set of switchbacks to avoid traversing slopes with greater avalanche potential along the upper reaches of the road.)

From the saddle, choose your line into the bowl to the north formed by the headwaters of Rainy Creek. You can climb back to the saddle directly, or find the Rainy Creek Road at about 3,900 feet and climb it to the east, switching back to the west at 4,200 feet to the saddle.

47 STEVENS PASS
Yodelin Summit
❄❄❄❄

Distance:	5.0 miles
Base elevation:	3,200 feet
Elevation gain:	2,000 feet
Trail time:	4.5 hours
Trail type:	Forest road, backcountry
Skill level:	Intermediate
Avalanche potential:	Moderate
Traction advisory:	Skins, waxless
Maps:	Green Trails 144; USGS Stevens Pass, Labyrinth Mountain (7.5' series)

Skyline Lake is west and across Highway 2 from Yodelin.

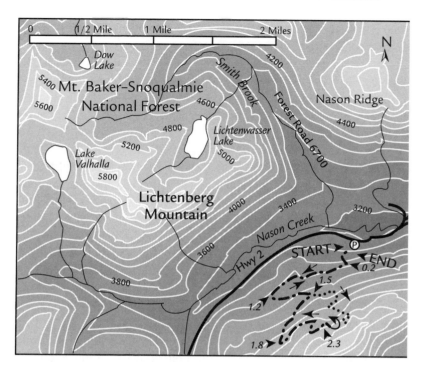

Getting There

From Seattle, follow I-5 north to US Highway 2, exit 194, and take US 2 east to Monroe. (Alternatively, take I-405 and State Route 522 to US 2 at Monroe.) From Monroe, follow US 2 to 3.3 miles east of Stevens Pass to a plowed parking area off the eastbound lanes. Allow about two hours for the drive from Seattle, and longer if you stop to put on chains.

The Route

0.0 Parking area
0.2 Road switches back and branches; follow upper switchback
0.4 Switchback
1.2 Switchback
1.5 Road switches back and branches; follow switchback to southwest
1.8 Switchback
2.3 Road ends; climb south to summit
2.5 Summit

Steep glades, open clear-cuts, and the cleared path of an old ski lift wait on the cold north side of a mile-high ridge that once served as the Yodelin ski area. An avalanche roared down on several winter homes on this north-facing slope in 1971, pretty much discouraging further development of the area.

Today, perhaps the only evidence of a lift at the site is the open lower slopes. A road crosses this slope, leading to higher country and runs through old forest and clear-cuts.

Climb on the road to a switchback at about 0.2 mile and 3,300 feet. Here the road forks at the switchback. Stay on the upper switchback, which then switches back to the west at about 0.4 mile. The road continues to climb westerly through clear-cut and old forest to another broad switchback at 3,700 feet and about 1.2 miles. At about 1.5 miles is a sharp switchback to the southwest again.

A spur road continues to contour east here, but follow the switchback another third of a mile to a final switchback east. The road climbs to an end at about 4,600 feet. This is the turnaround point for touring skiers. Those seeking their gravity fix can climb another fifth of a mile south-southeast to the 5,200-foot summit.

The best ride is directly north, crossing your tracks to the end of the road, then picking up clear-cuts and the clearing from the old lift as you descend.

Mission Ridge

High and dry is the best way to describe Mission Ridge, a lift-served snow-play area with excellent backcountry possibilities. Sunshine and light snow visit this area more frequently than they do other Cascade slopes, and it is often worth the drive for the increased chance of better weather.

The same factors that give Mission better snow and more sunshine also decrease the amount of snow the area gets. During winters of low snowpack, backcountry snowriders will have to choose their routes carefully.

The northern bowls off Mission Peak may be one area where you can ski or ride almost every winter. As for the Hog Loppet, you'll just have to read on.

48 MISSION RIDGE
Mission Peak
❄❄❄½

Distance:	2.0 miles
Base elevation:	6,700 feet
Elevation gain/loss:	200 feet/2,100 feet
Trail time:	2 to 6 hours
Trail type:	Ski trail, backcountry
Skill level:	Intermediate
Avalanche potential:	Moderate
Traction advisory:	Skins, waxless
Maps:	USGS Mission Peak (7.5' series)

Getting There

From Seattle, drive east on I-90 over Snoqualmie Pass to the easternmost Cle Elum exit, State Route 970, and follow the signs to Wenatchee. In 12 miles, SR 970 joins US Highway 97. Turn north here and follow US 97 past Blewett Pass to its junction with US 2. Follow US 2 east to Wenatchee and take the Wenatchee exit. Follow the signs through Wenatchee to the Mission Ridge ski area. Allow a total of about three and a half hours from Seattle; one and a half hours from Blewett Pass.

The Route

0.0 Mission Ridge ski area summit
0.5 Ski area boundary; turn left
1.0 Mission Peak

This route provides skiing and riding on the wild north and east faces of 6,875-foot Mission Peak, just outside the ski area boundary. You'll have to purchase a lift ticket for the short and easy way to the slopes; otherwise, plan on a long, three-hour, 2.3-mile climb from the ski area parking lot.

Backcountry skiers and riders who choose to ride the lifts can save their energy for the slope back down to the lodge at the end of the day. Those who choose to earn their turns can climb the slopes west of the lodge, first on a cat track that parallels the lower chairlift and then, as that track approaches the snowboard park, through the woods above.

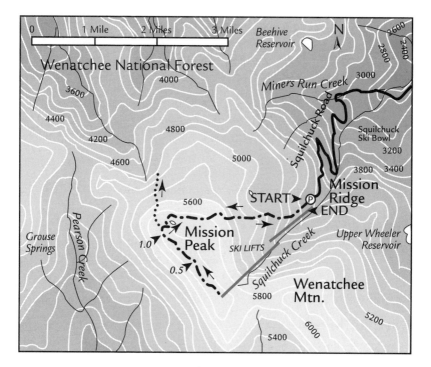

Continue climbing this forested ridge—glades here make excellent, seldom-tracked downhill riding in powder—between the ski area and the Lake Creek drainage to the north. The hill flattens at about 5,800 feet. Climb 100 feet over a knoll and continue climbing west-southwest to about 6,400 feet, where you will find a gently climbing ski run called Katsuk.

Ski up this run for 0.5 mile to join the route from the lifts. This is a long, steep climb, and most of the ski area runs back to the parking area are a real challenge for intermediate telemarkers.

Lift riders should turn right off the top lift and ski the flat Katsuk trail to the north. It traverses gently into forest north, then turns east at about 0.5 mile from the lift. Turn left here and leave the ski area boundary.

Ski into a broad valley called Cross-Country Park, aiming for a saddle to the north. Mission Peak is beyond, about a mile from the lift. From the summit, you can ski or ride northeast for about 500 vertical feet or cut through trees to the north to find open slopes that stretch down to about 5,600 feet.

The easiest return is to ski back to the ski area, or follow the climbing route into the forest and descend.

49 MISSION RIDGE
The Hog Loppet
½

Distance:	21.0 miles one way
Base elevation:	6,700 feet
Elevation gain/loss:	600 feet/1,600 feet
Trail time:	5 to 7 hours
Trail type:	Forest road, marked trail
Skill level:	Intermediate
Avalanche potential:	Low
Traction advisory:	Waxless, waxable, skating
Maps:	USGS Mission Peak, Swauk Pass (7.5' series); route map furnished by event organizers

Getting There

From Seattle, drive east on I-90 over Snoqualmie Pass to the easternmost Cle Elum exit, State Route 970, and follow the signs to Wenatchee. In 12 miles, SR 970 joins US Highway 97. Turn north here and follow US 97 past Blewett Pass to its junction with US 2. Follow US 2 east to Wenatchee and take the Wenatchee exit. Follow the signs through Wenatchee to the Mission Ridge ski area. Allow a total of about three and a half hours from Seattle; one and a half hours from Blewett Pass.

The Route

0.0 Mission Ridge ski area summit
4.5 First checkpoint
10.0 Second checkpoint
15.0 Haney Meadow checkpoint
21.0 Swauk Pass Sno-Park at Blewett Pass

If there ever was a fun way to take a 21-mile, one-way ski tour, the Hog Loppet has to be the way. Usually on the third Saturday in February, the Hog Loppet Association hosts the Hog Loppet, a fully supported cross-country ski event from Mission Ridge to Blewett Pass.

Hog Loppet is Swedish for "high lope," according to the organizers. "It isn't a race," they say, "until someone tries to pass you." The route is usually

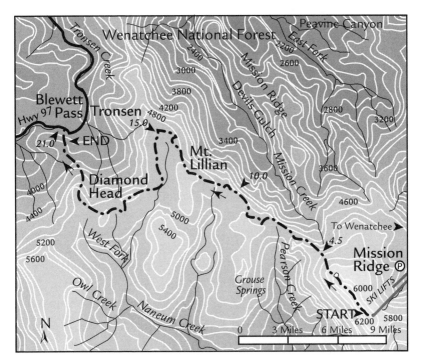

groomed well enough by local snowmobile clubs that skaters can enjoy the run and often do it in times so hot they melt the trail.

It's a beautiful tour and a great way to check out the splendid backcountry between Mission and Blewett—areas and slopes you can return to on long spring weekends. You begin by riding a bus to the Mission Ridge ski area and riding the lift to the summit. The race organizers provide the bus ride, for a $10 fee, from Wenatchee (where you leave your car) to the race start-point at Mission Ridge, and then back to Wenatchee from Blewett Pass at the end of the race.

Three checkpoints along the way are staffed by volunteers from local scouting organizations, snowmobile clubs, and the Chelan County Sheriff's Office. Besides spots to rest at the checkpoints, you'll find fresh fruit and trail snacks, water or energy drink, and, at Haney Meadow, a warming fire.

Most of the route is downhill, although you'll find several sections that climb 200 feet or more. The final climb is from Haney Meadow along Forest Road 9712, and it seems long because you've already not raced someone for at least 15 miles. The final 5 miles is moderately to gently downhill.

For more information, write to Hog Loppet, PO Box 2102, Wenatchee, WA 98807; or contact Asplund's Outdoor Sports in Wenatchee at (800) 922-2038.

The Okanogan

The light, dry snow of the Okanogan is the closest to the quality of Rocky Mountain white stuff that you'll find in the Cascades. The weather in this north-central part of the state is more likely to offer sunshine and clear, cold nights.

The price you pay for generally better snow and sunshine is measured in hours: It takes a long time to get to the Okanogan country. (The Okanogan, by the way, is another one of those geoetymological anomaly zones—British Columbians call it the Okanagan.) However you spell it, you've got to spend a long weekend here to do it any justice and much longer if you want to get to know some of the spots local snowriders don't often talk about in public.

You'll be sharing most of the ungroomed trails around the Okanogan with snowmobiles (or more accurately, they'll be sharing the trails with you). Except in the wilderness areas and on groomed trails reserved exclusively for cross-country skiers, there are probably more snowmobilers than skiers.

In fact, many backcountry snowriders rely on snowmobiles to take them to downhill areas that would otherwise be inaccessible. Harts Pass in the early spring, 33 miles northwest of Mazama, might be a good example.

You'll find four trails described here, one for family touring and three tough backcountry routes leading to steep downhill touched by skis or boards perhaps no more than two dozen times every winter. If you have the time, there's more than enough room for your tracks.

50 THE OKANOGAN
Loup Loup
❄

Distance:	1.0 to 10.0 miles
Base elevation:	3,900 feet
Elevation gain:	650 feet
Trail time:	1 to 4 hours
Trail type:	Forest roads
Skill level:	Novice
Avalanche potential:	None
Traction advisory:	Waxless, waxable
Maps:	Green Trails 85; USGS Loup Loup Summit (7.5' series)

Getting There

From Seattle, drive north on I-5 to Everett and US Highway 2, exit 194. Take US 2 east to Wenatchee. (An alternative route is to go north on I-405, then east on State Route 522 to Monroe, joining US 2 there.) From Wenatchee, follow Alt. US 97 north through Chelan to Pateros. Take SR 153 through Methow to Twisp. Drive 12 miles east of Twisp on SR 20 and turn right on Forest Road 41. Drive a third of a mile to the South Summit Sno-Park. Allow about five to six hours travel time from Seattle in winter.

The Route

0.0 Sno-Park
1.5 Second switchback on Forest Road 41
2.0 Hilltop (4,355 feet)

Various roads lead through the pine forests around 4,020-foot Loup Loup Pass. There's even a community ski area across the road, with a Poma lift and about 1,200 vertical feet of good hill.

On these tours, you'll be sticking to the south side of the highway, below the 4,655-foot Loup Loup Summit. Routes of up to 10 miles in length are groomed and marked for cross-country skiers, but if you follow well-marked forest roads through the pines, you'll find untracked, long-lasting powder in the trees.

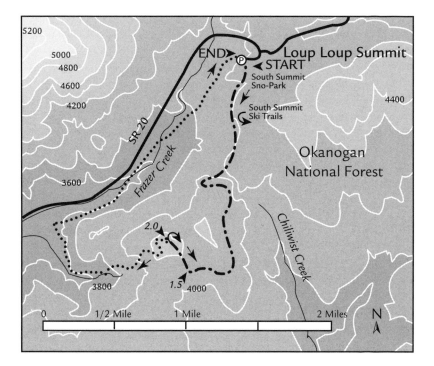

For some of the better downhill sections, follow Forest Road 41—the main road leading southerly into the woods from the Sno-Park—for about 1.5 miles around two switchbacks, climbing gently to about 4,100 feet. At the second switchback, leave the road and climb through the woods to the north-west and the top of a 4,355-foot hill.

You can descend through trees back to the road. Or you can drop into the west-facing bowl for a challenging tree run of about 700 vertical feet to FR 600, marked as Trail 10 and occasionally groomed. Turn right and follow this road down to a junction with FR 825, which parallels SR 20 back to the Sno-Park.

Families will enjoy the many touring possibilities here, and when Missy and Junior are ready for downhill thrills, they can visit Loup Loup Ski Bowl. The area is open Wednesdays and Fridays through Sundays.

51 | THE OKANOGAN
Silver Star Mountain

❄❄❄❄½

Distance:	7.2 miles
Base elevation:	3,400 feet
Elevation gain:	4,600 feet
Trail time:	8 hours
Trail type:	Backcountry
Skill level:	Advanced
Avalanche potential:	Considerable
Traction advisory:	Skins, waxless
Maps:	Green Trails 50; USGS Silver Star (15' series)

Lower slopes of Silver Star Mountain stretch above skiers on the Cutthroat Road.

Getting There

From Seattle, drive north on I-5 to Everett and US Highway 2, exit 194. Take US 2 east to Wenatchee. (An alternative route is to go north on I-405, then east on State Route 522 to Monroe, joining US 2 there.) From Wenatchee, follow Alt. US 97 north through Chelan to Pateros. Take SR 153 through Methow to Twisp. From Twisp, drive 11 miles north on SR 20 to Winthrop. From Winthrop, drive 21 miles northwest on SR 20 to the end of the plowed road at Silver Star Creek. (During winter, the highway is closed beyond this point.) Allow about five to six hours travel time from Seattle in winter.

The Route

0.0   Parking area
1.3   Creek crossing
2.1   West fork, Silver Star Creek; climb south
3.6   Silver Star Glacier

You owe the state Department of Transportation and the snowriders and snowmobilers of the Methow Valley many thanks for making this hill accessible to those of us who don't fly in helicopters during the winter. Several years ago, snowriders around the Methow Valley convinced the state that they could keep State Route 20 plowed all the way to the Silver Creek bridge, 7 miles beyond the spot where it once was gated at Mazama. Snowriders are delighted at the opportunity to reach the better snow and slopes of the high country.

From the parking area, climb into the forest above Silver Star Creek on the east side, first up a narrow ridge among pine and tamarack. Stay above the denser forest and steeper gully of the creek, following traces of a National Outdoor Leadership School way trail if possible.

At about 1.3 miles, after the creek valley flattens out, you can cross the creek at about 4,800 feet. Climb to the valley headwall at 5,200 feet, switching back if necessary.

At about 2.1 miles and 5,600 feet, you'll cross a gully formed by the west fork of Silver Star Creek. Make an ascending traverse from this point into the wide, open bowl formed by Silver Star Glacier, now underneath 10 to 20 feet of winter snow. Crevasses will not be a problem; avalanche is a much more real danger.

You can climb any of the three snowfields leading to the saddle between the east and west peaks of Silver Star. The easternmost snowfield is the widest

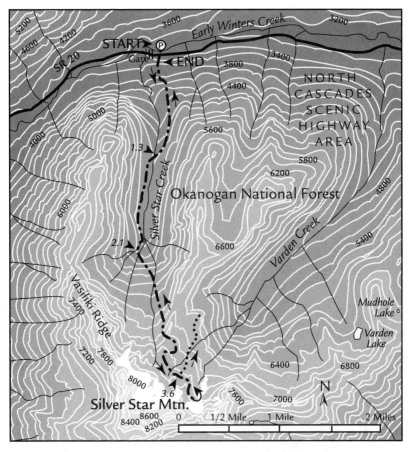

and is recommended here, while the steeper middle gully leads to an 8,600-foot saddle between the two summits.

Remember that these slopes face to the north and slide frequently during the winter months. If avalanche danger is anything but low, be extremely wary of the steeper sections of this route and be content with skiing the lower sections of the hill. After all, you've got more than 4,000 vertical feet in which to play.

52 THE OKANOGAN
Delancy Ridge
❄❄❄❄

Distance:	2.4 miles
Base elevation:	3,200 feet
Elevation gain:	2,800 feet
Trail time:	4 hours
Trail type:	Backcountry
Skill level:	Advanced
Avalanche potential:	Considerable
Traction advisory:	Skins
Maps:	Green Trails 50; USGS Silver Star, Mazama (7.5' series)

Delancy Ridge hides behind fog and a lone aspen.

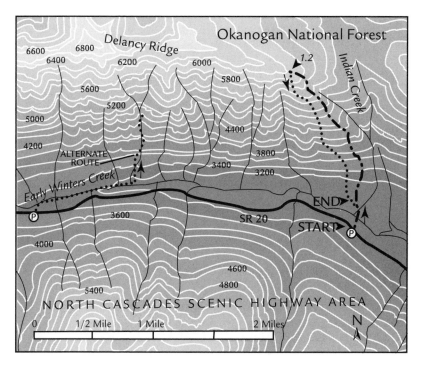

Getting There

From Seattle, drive north on I-5 to Everett and US Highway 2, exit 194. Take US 2 east to Wenatchee. (An alternative route is to go north on I-405, then east on State Route 522 to Monroe, joining US 2 there.) From Wenatchee, follow Alt. US 97 north through Chelan to Pateros. Take SR 153 through Methow to Twisp. From Twisp, drive 11 miles north on SR 20 to Winthrop. From Winthrop, drive 16 miles northwest on SR 20 and park to the right. Parking is also possible at the end of the plowed road, 21 miles northwest of Winthrop. Allow five to six hours travel time from Seattle in winter.

The Route

0.0 Parking
1.2 Ridge crest

Here is a straightforward climb that may appeal to boarders because of the many steep gullies and because you don't spend a lot of time slogging along the flats. You go up, you come down. You make a joyous noise. Then you do it again.

Delancy Ridge is the 7,000-foot wall to the immediate north of State Route 20 that leads west to the 8,200-foot Needles. You can climb it anywhere you think you can ride back down, with the open avalanche fans at the base of the ridge being the easiest. These lead to steeper chutes and gullies for riders seeking extreme thrills.

If you park along the road, drop down into the Early Winters Creek bed to the north. Cross at a snow bridge and climb any of the increasingly steep avalanche fans to the north.

If you park at the end of the plowed road at Silver Star Creek, cross the highway bridge just west of the spot where the road is closed and ski down the Klipchuck Campground Trail 522, which drops down the north side of Early Winters Creek underneath Delancy Ridge.

The eastern end of Delancy Ridge, above Klipchuck Campground, provides the most open slopes. Keep in mind that those avalanche fans were not caused by little trolls with snow shovels and avoid these areas in times of moderate to extreme avalanche danger.

53
THE OKANOGAN
Cutthroat Pass
❄❄❄❄

Distance:	15.6 miles
Base elevation:	3,400 feet
Elevation gain:	3,400 feet
Trail time:	9.5 hours
Trail type:	Highway, summer trail
Skill level:	Intermediate
Avalanche potential:	Considerable
Traction advisory:	Skins, waxless
Maps:	Green Trails 50; USGS Washington Pass (7.5' series)

Cutthroat Lake is just below the pass.

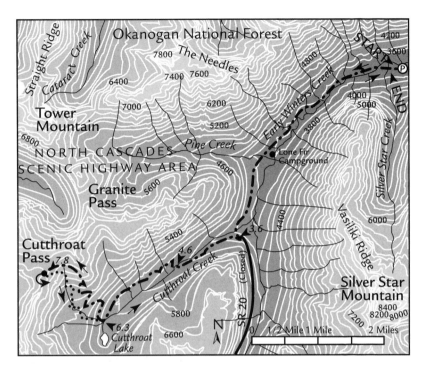

Getting There

From Seattle, drive north on I-5 to Everett and US Highway 2, exit 194. Take US 2 east to Wenatchee. (An alternative route is to go north on I-405, then east on State Route 522 to Monroe, joining US 2 there.) From Wenatchee, follow Alt. US 97 north through Chelan to Pateros. Take SR 153 through Methow to Twisp. From Twisp, drive 11 miles north on SR 20 to Winthrop. From Winthrop, drive 21 miles northwest on SR 20 to the end of the plowed road. (During winter, the highway is closed beyond this point.) Allow about five to six hours travel time from Seattle in winter.

The Route

0.0 Parking area
3.6 Cutthroat Creek Road; turn right
4.6 Cutthroat Lake trailhead
6.3 Cutthroat Lake Trail junction; climb right
7.8 Cutthroat Pass

This is another trip made possible by the people who keep State Route 20 plowed all the way to Silver Star Creek. You also owe a big thanks to Roy "Corduroy" Myers, who occasionally grooms the snow-covered highway and Cutthroat Creek Road, making the 5-mile tour up the road pass much faster.

Ski southwest on SR 20 about 3.6 miles to Cutthroat Creek Road. Turn right and follow Cutthroat Creek Road to the Cutthroat Lake trailhead. On cold, clear winter days, this section of the highway and road makes an excellent, scenic family tour.

From the trailhead at 4,500 feet, things get a bit more serious. Climb northwest from the trailhead, crossing Cutthroat Creek and climbing about 200 feet before switching back to the southwest to make an ascending traverse above the snow-covered Cutthroat Creek valley. Continue southwest to a junction with the Cutthroat Lake Trail at about 4,900 feet and 6.3 miles. (The lake lies in the basin about a quarter mile south.)

Turn northwest (right) from the junction and climb into the open bowl to the northwest at about 5,600 feet. Cutthroat Pass is the saddle in the ridge to the west-southwest, at the head of the bowl.

To reach it, climb up the east side of the bowl, traversing to the west at about 6,500 feet to gain the last 300 feet. If Corduroy's done his work, you probably have time for lunch and a look at the view—which is nothing short of exceeding anybody's community standards—before ripping off the skins and swooping 2,300 feet back to the trailhead.

Mount Baker

The area around the Mount Baker winter resort—which is actually closer to Mount Shuksan—probably challenges Mount Rainier for the quality of its snow and the quality, if not quantity, of its backcountry runs. Three of the best are outlined here, including one that is most easily reached by riding a ski lift. Purists can walk if they wish, remembering that even from the top of the lift, you've got to climb another 500 vertical feet.

54 MOUNT BAKER
Ptarmigan Ridge
❄❄❄❄

Distance: 10.0 miles
Base elevation: 4,100 feet
Elevation gain: 1,900 feet
Trail time: 6.5 hours
Trail type: Gravel road, summer trail
Skill level: Intermediate
Avalanche potential: Considerable
Traction advisory: Skins, waxable
Maps: Green Trails 13; USGS Mount Baker,
Shuksan Arm (7.5' series)

Getting There

From Seattle, take 1-5 north to Bellingham. From Bellingham, drive east on
State Route 542 about 60 miles to the upper parking area at the Mount Baker
winter resort. The road to the upper parking area may not be plowed on

Kulshan Ridge overlooks the route to Ptarmigan Ridge.

weekdays but is usually driven often enough that it is passable almost every day. Allow about three hours travel time from Seattle.

The Route

0.0 Upper parking lot
1.0 Austin Pass
2.1 Table Mountain saddle
4.0 Cross spur ridge
5.0 Camp Kiser

The bowls and open slopes around Ptarmigan Ridge provide downhill thrills of up to 1,200 vertical feet, and dedicated snowriders can start as early as November and continue around here on some hills until July.

From the parking area, climb up the groomed trail that forms the western edge of the Mount Baker winter resort. If you enjoy setting your own trail, climb on the ridge just to the west.

Climb south above the basin holding Bagley Lakes to the west, following traces of the road to 4,700-foot Austin Pass. From the pass, the route follows the ridgeline to the right, climbing and switching back above a wide bowl under Kulshan Ridge.

This bowl is an excellent alternative destination when the weather sucks, time is short, or the avalanche danger is considerable. You can find runs of about 400 vertical feet and even a cornice or two for air time along the north side of Kulshan Ridge.

You can switchback with the road or, from a swale about a quarter mile from Austin Pass, climb directly southwest to a flat spot just east of Table Mountain. From here, the route drops steeply off the ridge to the south about 200 feet, keeping in trees to avoid the open avalanche slopes below Table Mountain. These slopes should only be crossed in times of low avalanche danger—and then with caution.

A flatter valley floor leads west back up to a saddle on the west side of Table Mountain, at 2.1 miles. From here, you must cross another steep north-facing bowl to the more gentle Ptarmigan Ridge.

Once on Ptarmigan Ridge, follow the ridge on the southeast side, climbing steadily upward and eventually crossing a southern spur ridge at about 4.0 miles. From here, 6,414-foot Coleman Pinnacle—not easily confused with 10,778-foot Mount Baker looming behind—can be seen.

Camp Kiser, used as a base for climbers ascending Mount Baker from the southeast, is just west of Coleman Pinnacle. Stay along the southern side of

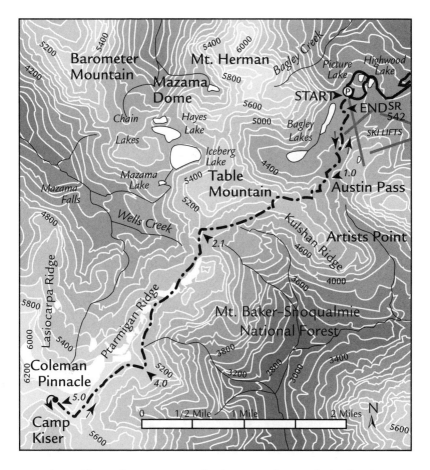

Ptarmigan Ridge and traverse around Coleman to the west-facing bowl. Steep, alpine-style runs are possible in powdered slopes facing virtually every direction.

Follow your tracks back to the saddle west of Table Mountain. An alternative route from here is to drop about 400 vertical feet to the north-northwest, then traverse north into the Iceberg Lake basin. Ski east between Iceberg and Hayes Lakes and climb 500 feet to Herman Saddle.

From here, follow the directions for Route 55, Herman Saddle, back to the parking lot. This route presents less avalanche danger but involves extra climbing.

55 MOUNT BAKER
Herman Saddle
❄❄❄

Distance:	5.0 miles
Base elevation:	4,100 feet
Elevation gain:	1,200 feet
Trail time:	3 hours
Trail type:	Summer trail
Skill level:	Intermediate
Avalanche potential:	Considerable
Traction advisory:	Skins, waxable
Maps:	Green Trails 14; USGS Mount Baker, Shuksan Arm (7.5' series)

Two skiers are dwarfed by the immense Herman Saddle.

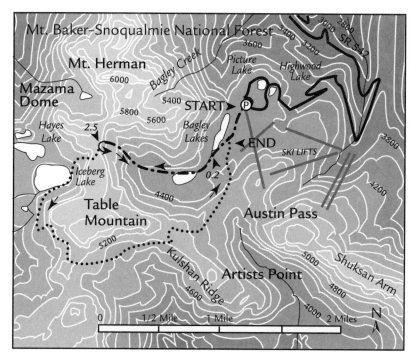

Getting There

From Seattle, take I-5 north to Bellingham. From Bellingham, drive east on State Route 542 about 60 miles to the upper parking area at the Mount Baker winter resort. The road to the upper parking area may not be plowed on weekdays but is usually driven often enough that it is passable almost every day. Allow about three hours travel time from Seattle.

The Route

0.0 Upper parking area
0.2 Bagley Lakes
2.5 Herman Saddle

With the exception of the lift-served Shuksan Arm, this is the most convenient backcountry snowriding around the Mount Baker area. You can ski the eastern bowl you climb or drop over the saddle to the west for a 500-vertical-foot ride down to the Chain Lakes. Or you can do both if you've been carbo-loading.

Start by climbing about a quarter mile south of the parking lot along the Blueberry cat track of the ski area, then drop about 100 feet down to Bagley

Lakes and ski southwest along this valley to the southwest of the lakes. Climb west up the valley and switchback up the headwall of the bowl to the north to about 4,600 feet before turning back to the west and climbing to the 5,300-foot saddle.

The run from the saddle drops off to the south before plunging west to the lakes below. Climb back to the saddle for the run down the other side or, if avalanche danger is low, climb around the west end of the lakes and Table Mountain to the ridge west of Table Mountain and follow the Ptarmigan Ridge route (Route 54) back to Austin Pass and the descent to the parking lot.

56 | MOUNT BAKER
Shuksan Arm

❄❄❄❄½

Distance:	1.0 to 3.0 miles
Base elevation:	3,500 feet
Elevation gain:	500 to 2,000 feet
Trail time:	1 to 4 hours
Trail type:	Backcountry
Skill level:	Advanced
Avalanche potential:	Moderate
Traction advisory:	Skins
Maps:	Green Trails 14; USGS Mount Baker,
	Shuksan Arm (7.5' series)

Getting There

From Seattle, take 1-5 north to Bellingham. From Bellingham, drive east on State Route 542 about 58 miles. Turn left onto White Salmon Day Lodge Road and follow it about three-quarters of a mile to the lodge parking area. Allow about three hours travel time from Seattle.

A skier crosses Bagley Lakes Basin.

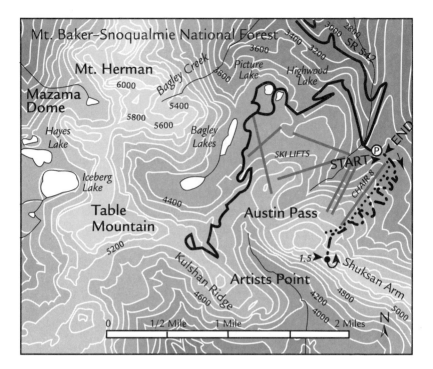

The Route

0.0 Parking area
1.0 Top of Chair 8
1.5 Shuksan Arm summit

Long before most telemark skiers had heard of Shuksan Arm, boarders were kicking steps up to the top of the peak above Chair 8 to carve big smiles in the ridge or test the narrow, steep gullies to the east. This is steep territory. Because it begins within the bounds of the ski area, snowriders should follow the rules posted on backcountry boundary signs at the top of the chairlift. Don't ride or ski out of bounds if the area is closed.

Begin by riding Chair 7 and taking the Otto Bahn run to the left. Ride Chair 8 to the top. The climbing begins just left of the chair lift and goes straight up the ridge to the summit.

The easiest run is back down the ridge. The more extreme hills are down the ridge and gully to the east of the ski area boundary, traversing back to the area at the base of Chair 8.

The Olympics

The Olympic Peninsula is largely overlooked by most snowriders, which is regarded as a happy circumstance by those who have found their own stash of powder around places like Hurricane Ridge or Deer Park—or the wild, silent slopes of the High Divide.

It is difficult to imagine that slopes so few miles from sea level might offer light snow. When you think of the Olympic Mountains, you are likely to picture the soggy rain forests of the Hoh River, not the mounds of white, light powder you'll explode when you swoop off the north side of Hurricane Hill.

At least once every winter, you should make a visit to the quiet side of Puget Sound and Hood Canal. But don't tell any of the locals where you heard about their stash.

Note: While exploding through this powder, you may notice a small cabin mentioned in several of the routes (see Route 63, Waterhole Trail). This cabin is owned by the National Park Service and is used to store emergency gear. It is open to users on a first-come, first-served basis, but the sign on the door states, "For emergency use only." There is no fee for its use, and use of it is common, despite the emergency warning.

57 THE OLYMPICS
Lodge Run
❄❄❄

Distance:	1.0 mile
Base elevation:	5,200 feet
Elevation loss:	600 feet
Trail time:	1 hour
Trail type:	Backcountry
Skill level:	Intermediate
Avalanche potential:	Moderate
Traction advisory:	Skins, waxless
Maps:	Green Trails 135; Custom Correct, Elwha Valley; USGS Mount Angeles (7.5' series)

A telemarker tests the ever-steepening slopes of the Lodge Run.

Getting There

From Seattle, first head toward the Hood Canal Bridge via one of two routes. Either take the ferry to Winslow on Bainbridge Island and drive up State Route 305 about 21 miles; or drive north on I-5 to Edmonds, and from there take the ferry to Kingston and drive west on SR 104 about 13 miles to the bridge. It's a little over an hour either way, but ferry lines can make the trip longer. From the bridge, drive west on SR 104 to US Highway 101 at Discovery Bay. Follow US 101 north and west through Sequim to Port Angeles. Turn left on Race Street and follow it past the Olympic National Park Visitor Center to the Hurricane Ridge Road. Follow the Hurricane Ridge Road 17 miles to Hurricane Ridge. Allow about two hours from the bridge to the ridge. Be prepared to pay a $10 per carload entrance fee on entering the park at Heart o' the Hills.

The road from Heart o' the Hills to Hurricane Ridge is frequently closed by bad weather, and during the past few winters it has only been plowed for weekend access. Park officials leave the road open through the week, however, if they don't have to plow. The gate at Heart o' the Hills is closed at dusk every night and usually opens by 10 A.M. The best advice is to telephone ahead for recorded road and weather information: (360) 452-0329.

The Route

0.0 Hurricane Ridge parking area
0.25 Turnaround point

Here's one of those jump-out-of-your-car-and-ride runs, which is literally true if you park on the south side of the parking lot. As with all winter outings at Hurricane Ridge, you should register at the lodge before hitting the slopes.

The lodge run starts on the south-facing slopes in front of the lodge and plunges over the brow of a hill that drops into a gully and infant tributary to the Lillian River.

The first part of this run, especially if you start on the west side of the lodge, is deceptively gentle. You'll drop about 150 feet before things begin to get interesting and the world drops out from underneath you.

Because the top is so flat and exposed, it is frequently windblown or suncrusted. This tends to discourage many snowriders, but those who continue down may find much better snow. If you ski or ride just west of the lodge,

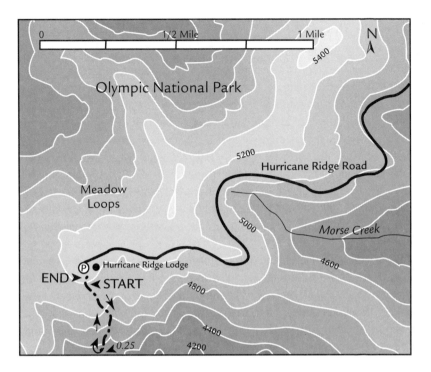

you'll probably get the longest ride to the south, with the last turns to the gully on a slope of about 40 degrees—about 600 vertical feet below the lodge.

It's less than a quarter mile to the bottom, but you'll switchback on the way up, adding at least three-quarters of a mile to the return.

58 | THE OLYMPICS
Toilet Bowl
❄❄❄

Distance:	1.8 miles
Base elevation:	5,200 feet
Elevation loss:	Up to 800 feet
Trail time:	2 hours
Trail type:	Road, backcountry
Skill level:	Intermediate
Avalanche potential:	Moderate
Traction advisory:	Skins, waxable
Maps:	Green Trails 134, 135; Custom Correct, Elwha Valley; USGS Mount Angeles, Hurricane Hill (7.5' series)

Sun crust challenges skiers on the south side of Toilet Bowl.

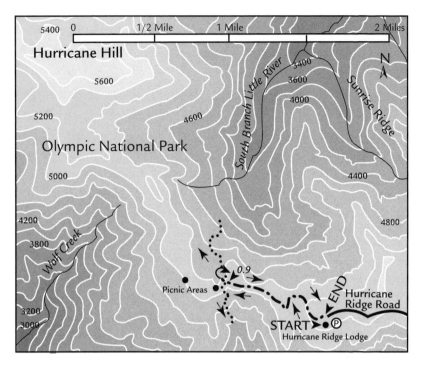

Getting There

From Seattle, first head toward the Hood Canal Bridge via one of two routes. Either take the ferry to Winslow on Bainbridge Island and drive up State Route 305 about 21 miles; or drive north on I-5 to Edmonds, and from there take the ferry to Kingston and drive west on SR 104 about 13 miles to the bridge. It's a little over an hour either way, but ferry lines can make the trip longer. From the bridge, drive west on SR 104 to US Highway 101 at Discovery Bay. Follow US 101 north and west through Sequim to Port Angeles. Turn left on Race Street and follow it past the Olympic National Park Visitor Center to the Hurricane Ridge Road. Follow the Hurricane Ridge Road 17 miles to Hurricane Ridge. Allow about two hours from the bridge to the ridge. Be prepared to pay a $10 per carload entrance fee on entering the park at Heart o' the Hills.

For information about snow and driving conditions from Heart o' the Hills to Hurricane Ridge, see the Getting There section for Route 57, Lodge Run.

The Route

0.0   Hurricane Ridge parking area
0.9   Toilet Bowl

The name of this run will become obvious if you drop too fast off the road that leads to it and you smack into a concrete building with doors that read MEN and WOMEN. This is an interesting hill, especially in the spring when you can ski the corn of the south-facing slopes and the powder of the north bowl.

Walk to the west end of the parking area just past the lodge, where you can step into your skis. Riders may want to walk another 100 yards west to the point where the road to Hurricane Hill begins to drop to the north. This gentle downhill is good practice for beginning cross-country skiers learning the snowplow or straight downhill running.

The hill drops gently to the north for about a quarter mile, then flattens out and turns west before veering sharply northwest. There's a steep but short run into the trees to the west and a great view of Mount Carrie and the Bailey Range from here.

The road drops again for about another quarter mile before a gentle, short climb and then descent to Toilet Bowl. There's a short, flat entry to the north bowl over snowdrifts. Ski or ride past windblown trees to the south to the wide, open meadow, which on sunny spring days gives you a glorious ride of about 500 vertical feet before trees and a gully make further progress difficult.

Trees in the upper part of the north bowl may discourage some skiers, but the 100-foot drop to the flat meadow below is only part of the run. Ski through the trees in the basin to the north to find a steep, open slope that drops about 700 vertical feet before you encounter timberline.

Before starting down, remember the First Law of the Great Telemalarky (a minor Norse deity with double-jointed knees): Gravity sucks. This means, of course, a whole lot of fun going down and a whole lot of work climbing back.

59 THE OLYMPICS
Wolf Creek Trail
❄❄

Distance:	8.7 miles one way
Base elevation:	5,200 feet
Elevation loss:	4,000 feet
Trail time:	4 hours
Trail type:	Abandoned road
Skill level:	Intermediate
Avalanche potential:	Low
Traction advisory:	Waxless, waxable
Maps:	Green Trails 134; Custom Correct, Elwha Valley; USGS Mount Angeles, Hurricane Hill (7.5' series)

The snow-covered road from Hurricane Ridge lodge leads to the Wolf Creek Trail.

Getting There

This downhill route from Hurricane Ridge to Whiskey Bend on the Elwha River requires two cars for everyone except those who are part helicopter. You need to leave one car at the Whiskey Bend trailhead on the Elwha River. From Seattle, first head toward the Hood Canal Bridge via one of two routes. Either take the ferry to Winslow on Bainbridge Island and drive up State Route 305 about 21 miles; or drive north on I-5 to Edmonds, and from there take the ferry to Kingston and drive west on SR 104 about 13 miles to the bridge. It's a little over an hour either way, but ferry lines can make the trip longer. From the bridge, drive west on SR 104 to US Highway 101 at Discovery Bay. Follow US 101 north and west through Sequim to Port Angeles. Turn left on Race Street to bypass the downtown area. Follow Race Street to Lauridsen Boulevard and turn right. Lauridsen leads west back to US 101 and the western outskirts of the city.

Turn left on US 101 and follow it 9 miles to the Elwha River Road. Turn left on the Elwha River Road, noting its intersection with the Little River Road after about a tenth of a mile, and follow the Elwha River Road past the Olympic National Park entrance station. If the station is open, you'll be asked to pay a $10 per carload entrance fee. Pay for one car and take the pass, which is good for seven days, in the second car after leaving the first at Whiskey Bend. (If the fee booth is closed, as it may be in the winter, simply continue on your way.)

Stay on the Elwha River Road, and turn left on Whiskey Bend Road just past the Elwha Ranger Station. Follow the winding, gravel road for 5 miles to the trailhead parking lot.

Now everyone climb in the second car and drive to Hurricane Ridge. (For information about snow and driving conditions from Heart o' the Hills to Hurricane Ridge, see the Getting There section for Route 57, Lodge Run.) During most winters, you can take a shortcut by turning right on the Little River Road. This gravel road climbs up to Lake Dawn, where it joins the Hurricane Ridge Road just below Heart o' the Hills, where you will probably be asked to pay $10 per carload or to show the pass you bought at the Elwha. Turn right on Hurricane Ridge Road and follow it to snow country. Allow three to four hours travel time from Seattle.

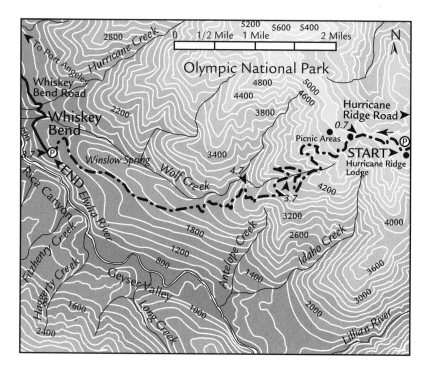

The Route

- **0.0** Hurricane Ridge parking area
- **0.7** Wolf Creek Trail; turn left
- **3.7** Third Wolf Creek crossing
- **4.7** Switchback above Wolf Creek
- **8.7** Whiskey Bend trailhead

In most winters, you'll be walking the lower three and a half miles of this abandoned road, which was once the only way to drive to Hurricane Ridge. The story goes that when the road was built, crews starting on the Elwha River met with crews starting at Hurricane Ridge at Whiskey Bend, where they shared the bottle that gave the place its name.

This is a good tour for those who enjoy long stretches of downhill trail, great views, and solitude. Those who have not arranged for a second car can plan to turn around after a few miles to ski back up the road to Hurricane Ridge.

Begin by skiing west of the parking lot on the snow-covered Hurricane Hill Road. Ski the road to the Wolf Creek Trail, marked by a sign and perhaps gateposts to the left of the road.

Follow the trail down as it traverses a broad, open hill below a picnic area and Toilet Bowl. This hill makes the best downhill run (and is described in Route 58, Toilet Bowl). The trail can be picked up in the trees on the west end of the slope.

The route turns and switches back at about 4,300 feet to make the first of three crossings of snow-covered Wolf Creek. The trail turns west again to drop steeply along the ridge above the creek and switches back to cross the creek again at 3,700 feet.

Continue dropping on the road, now in the forest, to another switchback and the third crossing of Wolf Creek at about 3,500 feet and 3.7 miles. If you plan to ski back to Hurricane Ridge, this might be the spot to turn around. In most winters, snow beyond this point can be spotty.

Those with a car at Whiskey Bend will probably remove their skis and walk down the road as the forest gathers around them, first through smaller trees and later through old-growth fir. The last 2 miles of road traverse hillside covered with evergreens and, later, huge maples before rounding a wide switchback just above Whiskey Bend and passing an old horse corral just before the parking lot.

You can also travel the other way on this route, of course—from Whiskey Bend up to Hurricane Ridge. This route to Hurricane is a good outing for a long weekend when, as sometimes happens, Hurricane Ridge Road is closed by storms. You can backpack to a snowline camp and ski up Wolf Creek Trail to downhill thrills around Hurricane Hill (see Route 60).

THE OLYMPICS

60 Hurricane Hill

❄❄❄❄½

Distance:	6.0 miles
Base elevation:	5,200 feet
Elevation gain:	800 feet
Trail time:	4 hours
Trail type:	Road, summer trail, backcountry
Skill level:	Intermediate
Avalanche potential:	Considerable
Traction advisory:	Skins, waxable
Maps:	Green Trails 134; Custom Correct, Elwha Valley; USGS Mount Angeles, Hurricane Hill (7.5' series)

The wide southeast bowl of Hurricane Hill always has untracked snow.

Getting There

From Seattle, first head toward the Hood Canal Bridge via one of two routes. Either take the ferry to Winslow on Bainbridge Island and drive up State Route 305 about 21 miles; or drive north on I-5 to Edmonds, and from there take the ferry to Kingston and drive west on SR 104 about 13 miles to the bridge. It's a little over an hour either way, but ferry lines can make the trip longer. From the bridge, drive west on SR 104 to US Highway 101 at Discovery Bay. Follow US 101 north and west through Sequim to Port Angeles. Turn left on Race Street and follow it past the Olympic National Park Visitor Center to the Hurricane Ridge Road. Follow the Hurricane Ridge Road 17 miles to Hurricane Ridge. Allow about 2 hours from the bridge to the ridge. Be prepared to pay a $10 per carload entrance fee on entering the park at Heart o' the Hills.

For information about snow and driving conditions from Heart o' the Hills to Hurricane Ridge, see the Getting There section for Route 57, Lodge Run.

The Route

- **0.0** Hurricane Ridge parking area
- **0.9** Toilet Bowl
- **1.3** Road ends
- **1.5** Steep and Icy; climb right
- **2.1** Little River Trail
- **2.7** Hurricane Hill Trail; climb right
- **3.0** Hurricane Hill summit

At 5,757 feet high, Hurricane Hill has something to offer all snowriders. Boarders and telemarkers who plod the road and trail will be rewarded by a steep, wide-open bowl and even steeper north-facing glades and with runs up to 1,700 vertical feet. Cross-country skiers will enjoy the spectacular views of Mount Carrie, the Bailey Range, and the home of the gods, Mount Olympus.

After registering at the lodge, ski west on the Hurricane Hill Road, resisting the temptation to turn downhill at Toilet Bowl. Continue past Toilet Bowl and up a gentle hill to the end of the road at about 1.3 miles.

From this point, the paved nature trail underneath the snow drops gently to a broad saddle before traversing under the west side of a steep 5,500-foot peak. There are two routes possible from this point: up and over the peak, or around the west ridge to a spot called Steep and Icy.

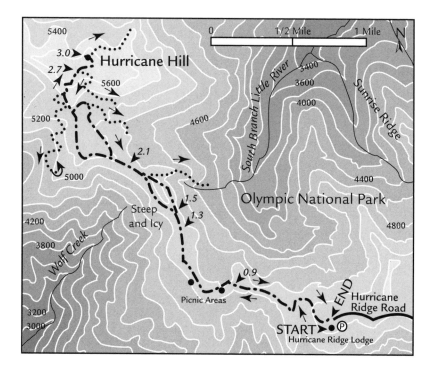

It is aptly named, with an exposed slope that exceeds 40 degrees at the shoulder of the ridge. Steep and Icy is one of those places where you begin to appreciate full-length steel edges on your skis.

The more comfortable route is up and over the peak. From the saddle, climb to the northwest, keeping away from the northeast-facing cornices that may form along the crest of the peak. Orange poles may be placed along this section to guide you, and cross-country skiers may find that carrying their skis is easier than switching back. Those with skins can climb most of the hill without switchbacks.

Drop down the hill to the northwest to a 5,073-foot saddle, where you rejoin the trail exiting Steep and Icy. A humongous cornice sometimes forms on this saddle, at just about the point where in the summer the Little River Trail drops off to the north.

Just beyond this saddle, another choice of routes is possible. When the snow is stable, you can climb about 50 vertical feet along the trail, then cross the ridge to the northeast, traversing underneath cornices menacing above.

The danger is passed quickly, however, and this route leads to the splendid glades that form the lower Hurricane Hill Bowl. It is possible to ride about 350 vertical feet on sheltered, powder-miser north-facing slopes, out of the wind that often scours Hurricane Hill.

Those bound for the summit of Hurricane Hill can climb into the vast open bowl to the northwest below Hurricane Hill, aiming for an obvious saddle where you rejoin the trail to the summit.

When there's any doubt about snow stability, follow the trail as it climbs on the west side of the ridge around to a saddle at 2.7 miles, where a trail leads west to the Elwha River Valley. From the saddle, the trail switches back right up the broad, wide-open slope to the north-northeast, turning east to the summit.

The summit was the site of a World War II aircraft-spotter lookout, and cable anchors that held it to the top of the mountain may still be seen in the summer. Herb Crisler, who filmed the Disney nature movie, *Olympic Elk*, wintered in the lookout one year and his wife, Lois, wrote of marmots emerging sleepy and soggy to greet the spring sunshine on the slopes below.

Once you're rested, the slopes below should be enough to give you a double ibuprofen night. When conditions are stable, test the steep bowl to the north of the summit for open or gladed runs of 800 vertical feet. The sunny southwest-facing slope you climbed starts out gently but becomes increasingly steep as you plunge as much as 1,700 vertical feet down a gully and tributary to Wolf Creek.

Most snowriders find that the bowl to the southeast is enough exercise for them, beginning from the summit for the steepest runs or following their uphill tracks to the saddle where the two routes meet, then dropping off into the bowl where it is more gentle.

Another excellent north-facing bowl can be found by skiing west from the saddle about a quarter mile. A summer trail snakes along the Hurricane Hill ridge here, eventually dropping steeply to the Elwha Ranger Station 4,000 feet below.

61 THE OLYMPICS
Mount Angeles
❄❄❄½

Distance:	2.0 miles
Base elevation:	5,200 feet
Elevation gain:	250 feet
Trail time:	1 hour
Trail type:	Summer trail, backcountry
Skill level:	Intermediate
Avalanche potential:	Moderate
Traction advisory:	Skins, waxable
Maps:	Green Trails 135; Custom Correct, Elwha Valley; USGS Mount Angeles (7.5' series)

Mount Angeles plays hide-and-seek with clouds.

Getting There

From Seattle, first head toward the Hood Canal Bridge via one of two routes. Either take the ferry to Winslow on Bainbridge Island and drive up State Route 305 about 21 miles; or drive north on I-5 to Edmonds, and from there take the ferry to Kingston and drive west on SR 104 about 13 miles to the bridge. It's a little over an hour either way, but ferry lines can make the trip longer. From the bridge, drive west on SR 104 to US Highway 101 at Discovery Bay. Follow US 101 north and west through Sequim to Port Angeles. Turn left on Race Street and follow it past the Olympic National Park Visitor Center to the Hurricane Ridge Road. Follow the Hurricane Ridge Road 17 miles to Hurricane Ridge. Allow about two hours from the bridge to the ridge. Be prepared to pay a $10 per carload entrance fee on entering the park at Heart o' the Hills.

For information about snow and driving conditions from Heart o' the Hills to Hurricane Ridge, see the Getting There section for Route 57, Lodge Run.

The Route

0.0 Hurricane Ridge parking area
0.2 Top of rope tow
0.6 Open meadow
1.0 Hurricane Ridge Road

The downhill rush on this run starts about 0.6 mile northeast of the parking area in an open meadow. Here, a summer trail traverses underneath Mount Angeles to Klahhane Ridge. From there, it drops in steep, open meadows and glades to the Hurricane Ridge Road, about 600 feet below.

From the parking area, climb northeast along the edge of the ski runs from the upper rope tow. Follow the crest of the ridge to the northeast, dropping in trees to the west if necessary to avoid gnarly drift bumps that the less sane of you may wish to jump.

Traverse to the right of the next ridge at about 5,200 feet for about a quarter mile, and at the saddle, look down the increasingly steep gully. The road is at the bottom of the gully, but can't be seen. Ski down the gully and exit around trees to the right.

Return to the ridge parking area by walking up the road or switching back to the saddle.

Snowriders can also continue along the top of the ridge for another mile to the saddle just south of the rocky summit block of 6,454-foot Mount

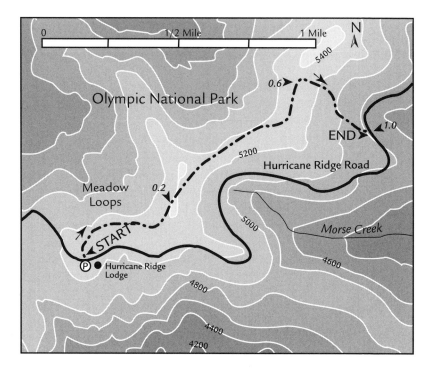

Angeles at 5,250 feet. Climb north up the ridge to about 5,500 feet, then traverse northwest into meadows that drop to the west underneath the summit. These meadows make good runs of about 400 vertical feet.

Ski mountaineers can climb farther north-northwest to a wide, open slope that leads north to a saddle just below the summit. This steep hill can be climbed and descended when conditions permit.

62

THE OLYMPICS
Klahhane Ridge
❄❄❄❄

Distance:	2.0 miles
Base elevation:	4,500 feet
Elevation gain:	1,400 feet
Trail time:	2.5 hours
Trail type:	Summer trail, backcountry
Skill level:	Advanced
Avalanche potential:	Considerable
Traction advisory:	Skins, waxless
Maps:	Green Trails 135; Custom Correct, Elwha Valley; USGS Mount Angeles, Port Angeles (7.5' series)

Getting There

From Seattle, first head toward the Hood Canal Bridge via one of two routes. Either take the ferry to Winslow on Bainbridge Island and drive up State Route 305 about 21 miles; or drive north on I-5 to Edmonds, and from there take the ferry to Kingston and drive west on SR 104 about 13 miles to the bridge. It's a little over an hour either way, but ferry lines can make the trip longer. From the bridge, drive west on SR 104 to US Highway 101 at Discovery Bay. Follow US 101 north and west through Sequim to Port Angeles. Turn left on Race Street and follow it past the Olympic National Park Visitor Center to the Hurricane Ridge Road. Follow the Hurricane Ridge Road 17 miles to Hurricane Ridge. Allow about two hours from the bridge to the ridge. Be prepared to pay a $10 per carload entrance fee on entering the park at Heart o' the Hills.

Park at the plowed area off the road 2 miles north of the Hurricane Ridge lodge at about 4,500 feet and walk up the road about a third of a mile to a hairpin corner and gully that climbs north to the summit of Mount Angeles. The hairpin may also have a plowed area for parking. The summer Switchback Trail starts at this hairpin, although with adequate snow cover, there's little point in trying to follow it.

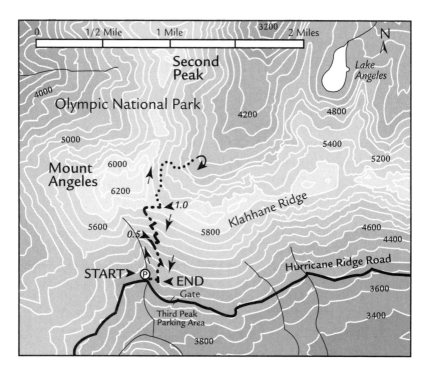

For information about snow and driving conditions from Heart o' the Hills to Hurricane Ridge, see the Getting There section for Route 57, Lodge Run.

The Route

0.0 Hairpin corner
0.5 Mount Angeles Trail junction; climb right
1.0 Klahhane saddle

This is a no-nonsense climb to a 5,900-foot saddle east-southeast of Mount Angeles that offers a steep ride back to the road or a 500-vertical-foot bowl to the north when conditions permit. Cross-country skiers will probably have more fun on Route 63, Waterhole Trail. But gravity freaks would be hard-pressed to find a better hill. You know who you are.

Don't waste time switching back. In fact, if the snow is consolidated enough, you can carry skis or board and kick steps up the steep hill.

Climb up the gully about 200 yards, then turn right and climb the steep slope that confronts you. Continue to climb 500 vertical feet in about 0.5 mile to a junction with the Mount Angeles Trail. The trail to the left leads to

Hurricane Ridge in 2.5 miles. To the right, switching back through increasingly open slopes, is the route to Klahhane Ridge.

Keep climbing to the right, and in another 500 vertical feet you'll strike the Klahhane Ridge saddle. A summer trail leads along the ridge to the northeast to Lake Angeles and then plunges into the bowl to the north to First Peak and eventually Heart o' the Hills.

Most folks pause on this high saddle to admire the view. Mountains sprout everywhere. You can look south to Long Ridge and beyond, the Bailey Range, and endless peaks toward Mount Anderson. The Needles gouge clouds to the east, and Vancouver Island floats across the Strait of Juan de Fuca to the north.

The saddle is often free of snow, thanks in large part to the winds that give Hurricane Ridge its name. It is one reason mountain goats wintered here prior to the park purge.

If time and conditions permit, drop into the bowl to the north, swooping at least 500 vertical feet to tree line. If powder is to be found anywhere in the Olympics, it is to be found here.

The ride back down to the road is also excellent in midwinter when snow depths permit. Lower portions of the route may be cleaned by slides or spring melt.

63

THE OLYMPICS
Waterhole Trail
❋❋❋

Distance:	8.0 miles
Base elevation:	5,200 feet
Elevation loss:	400 feet
Trail time:	4 hours
Trail type:	Gravel road
Skill level:	Novice
Avalanche potential:	Low
Traction advisory:	Waxless, waxable
Maps:	Green Trails 135; Custom Correct, Elwha Valley; USGS Mount Angeles (7.5' series)

Waterhole Trail traverses below Hurricane Ridge Road, under Steeple Rock, right.

Getting There

From Seattle, first head toward the Hood Canal Bridge via one of two routes. Either take the ferry to Winslow on Bainbridge Island and drive up State Route 305 about 21 miles; or drive north on I-5 to Edmonds, and from there take the ferry to Kingston and drive west on SR 104 about 13 miles to the bridge. It's a little over an hour either way, but ferry lines can make the trip longer. From the bridge, drive west on SR 104 to US Highway 101 at Discovery Bay. Follow US 101 north and west through Sequim to Port Angeles. Turn left on Race Street and follow it past the Olympic National Park Visitor Center to the Hurricane Ridge Road. Follow the Hurricane Ridge Road 17 miles to Hurricane Ridge. Allow about two hours from the bridge to the ridge. Be prepared to pay a $10 per carload entrance fee on entering the park at Heart o' the Hills.

For information about snow and driving conditions from Heart o' the Hills to Hurricane Ridge, see the Getting There section for Route 57, Lodge Run.

The Route

0.0 Hurricane Ridge parking area
0.5 Cutoff junction; turn right
0.7 Cox Valley trailhead
1.7 Open saddle
2.0 Steeple Rock
4.0 Waterhole cabin

The route begins down Obstruction Point Road, from the southeast end of the Hurricane Ridge parking lot, just past the trailer used as a lift ticket booth at the ridge. The first half mile is steep and exposed. This daunting beginning to a fine tour through woods to eye-popping views and steep, open riding slopes can be avoided by walking from the parking lot back down the Hurricane Ridge Road for 0.5 mile to the first hairpin corner to the left. Climb the bank to the southeast and posthole, ski, ride, or glissade to Obstruction Point Road, visible at tree line below. This 200-vertical-foot hill is usually too cruddy from postholing for good skiing or riding, but if you're first to try it after a storm, it can be an excellent slide.

The two routes join each other at about 0.7 mile (at the Cox Valley trailhead), and the road begins to descend more gently into a ridgetop forest. Snow on this wide ridge hides the Obstruction Point Road, which once was intended to connect with the Deer Park Road, about 17 miles to the east.

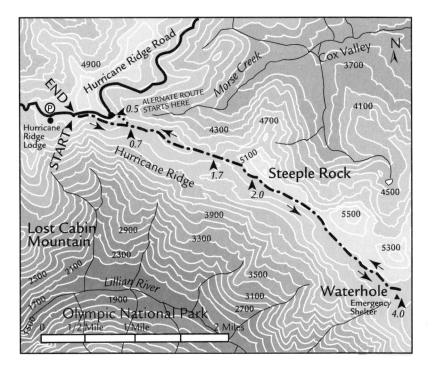

Continue through the forest, first gently up, then gently down as the road switches back onto an open saddle at about 1.7 miles. This saddle might be a good lunch or turnaround spot for families or novice skiers who can see the steeper, open route in front of them leading to Steeple Rock.

Those wishing to continue are likely to find icy, hardpacked slopes for about a third of a mile as the road climbs to a steep meadow beneath Steeple Rock. The southwest face of this meadow offers open snowriding of about 500 vertical feet when conditions permit.

The road traverses around Steeple Rock, climbing to about 5,100 feet as it follows the ridge. It is difficult to imagine the view from Hurricane Ridge getting any better—but if it does, the open ridge past Steeple Rock may offer it. Look south up the wide Elwha Valley and west to the Bailey Range and Mount Olympus.

The road enters the forest again and the last mile to Waterhole is along a flat, sheltered section that frequently provides enjoyable kick-and-glide powder that sparkles with surface hoar. Waterhole is a forested swale where a summer trail drops to tiny P. J. Lake to the northeast.

To the southwest, only a couple of hundred yards through the woods, explorers may happen on a cute little A-frame cabin that sleeps about six, complete with woodstove, cooking utensils, and plenty of dry wood under the floor. This cabin is maintained in the winter by a local ski club and the Park Service as an emergency shelter, and it is surprising how many emergencies pop up on weekends in this wilderness.

The best downhill opportunities around Waterhole will be found by continuing up the road and climbing 6,247-foot Eagle Point. On the way home from Waterhole, cross-country skiers will enjoy the run down the road and the thrill of attempting to stay in control while trying to decide whether to watch the view or the road ahead on the section around Steeple Rock.

64

THE OLYMPICS
Obstruction Point
❄❄❄

Distance:	15.8 miles
Base elevation:	5,200 feet
Elevation gain:	1,200 feet
Trail time:	8 hours
Trail type:	Gravel road
Skill level:	Intermediate
Avalanche potential:	Moderate
Traction advisory:	Waxless, waxable
Maps:	Green Trails 135; Custom Correct, Elwha Valley; USGS Mount Angeles, Maiden Peak (7.5' series)

Eagle Point, right, is the 6-mile mark on the Obstruction Point Road.

Getting There

From Seattle, first head toward the Hood Canal Bridge via one of two routes. Either take the ferry to Winslow on Bainbridge Island and drive up State Route 305 about 21 miles; or drive north on I-5 to Edmonds, and from there take the ferry to Kingston and drive west on SR 104 about 13 miles to the bridge. It's a little over an hour either way, but ferry lines can make the trip longer. From the bridge, drive west on SR 104 to US Highway 101 at Discovery Bay. Follow US 101 north and west through Sequim to Port Angeles. Turn left on Race Street and follow it past the Olympic National Park Visitor Center to the Hurricane Ridge Road. Follow the Hurricane Ridge Road 17 miles to Hurricane Ridge. Allow about two hours from the bridge to the ridge. Be prepared to pay a $10 per carload entrance fee on entering the park at Heart o' the Hills.

For information about snow and driving conditions from Heart o' the Hills to Hurricane Ridge, see the Getting There section for Route 57, Lodge Run.

The Route

0.0 Hurricane Ridge parking area
4.0 Waterhole
5.8 Eagle Point
7.9 Obstruction Point

Strong snowriders can enjoy the open alpine slopes of Eagle Point and beyond by continuing past Waterhole (see Route 63) to Obstruction Point. This makes a long day-tour—or in an emergency, you may be able to stay in the Waterhole cabin, provided someone hasn't already had an emergency there.

Cross-country skiers intimidated by the distance on this trip may find encouragement by knowing that Jack Hughes, the venerable Hurricane Ridge ranger, has skied the entire route and back in under three hours. Jack Hughes is older than most ice in the Blue Glacier.

From Waterhole, the road climbs steeply for about a half mile past steep, open slopes sweeping down from Eagle Point above to a switchback. Cross-country skiers can follow the road, and downhillers with skins can climb the broad, open slope to the northeast, connecting with the road 200 feet above. Eagle Point is another 500 vertical feet above and offers a steep, north-facing challenge for downhillers who are willing to ski or snowshoe the distance to reach the slope.

Beyond Eagle Point, the road alternately climbs and drops through alpine meadows, following the crest of a ridge to the southeast. It rounds Obstruction

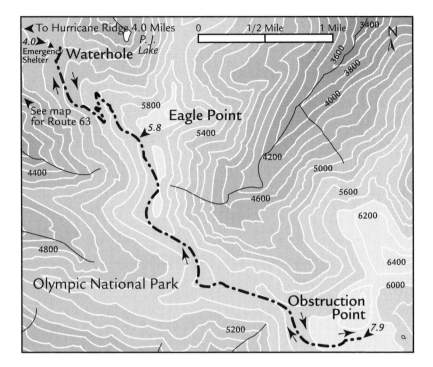

Point through a glade of alpine fir to the south, just beyond a flat saddle and views of Victoria, B.C., and Vancouver Island to the north.

Campers and strong snowriders with time will want to test the open slopes to the southwest from the broad summit of a 6,300-foot hill just southeast of the area that is used as the Obstruction Point parking lot when it's not snow-covered. These slopes drop to a tiny unnamed lake about 500 feet below.

When conditions permit, there's a 1,000-vertical foot run to the east from the summit of 6,450-foot Obstruction Point, just west of the parking lot. This run is extreme backcountry downhilling at its finest, offering eminently huck-able cliffs. Obstruction may also be descended to the west in a 900-vertical-foot bowl—but both of these runs are swept by avalanches and you should be very cautious in testing these slopes, else you'll have a real emergency on your hands.

Several summer trails lead from Obstruction Point to fine wilderness snowriding, but are beyond the range of most day-trippers. If you are snow-camping or staying at Waterhole, try following the ridge southeast along the route of the Grand Lake Trail, where you'll find three steep northeast-facing bowls into Badger Valley up to 1,600 vertical feet.

65 THE OLYMPICS
Second Peak

❄❄❄

Distance:	8.2 miles
Base elevation:	1,900 feet
Elevation gain:	4,100 feet
Trail time:	7 hours
Trail type:	Summer trail
Skill level:	Intermediate
Avalanche potential:	Low
Traction advisory:	Skins, waxable
Maps:	Green Trails 103; Custom Correct, Elwha Valley; USGS Port Angeles, Mount Angeles (7.5' series)

Getting There

From Seattle, first head toward the Hood Canal Bridge via one of two routes. Either take the ferry to Winslow on Bainbridge Island and drive up State Route 305 about 21 miles; or drive north on I-5 to Edmonds, and from there take the ferry to Kingston and drive west on SR 104 about 13 miles to the bridge. It's a little over an hour either way, but ferry lines can make the trip longer. From the bridge, drive west on SR 104 to US Highway 101 at Discovery Bay. Follow US 101 north and west through Sequim to Port Angeles. Turn left on Race Street and follow it past the Olympic National Park Visitor Center to the Hurricane Ridge Road. About 100 yards before passing through the park entrance booth at Heart o' the Hills, turn right up a hill on a park road past staff housing to a parking lot that may or may not be plowed. If not, park in the small lot next to the phone booth and entrance station and walk or ski back to the trailhead. Allow about two hours from the bridge to the ridge.

The Route

0.0 Parking lot
1.5 Halfway Rock
3.0 Heather Park
4.1 Second Peak

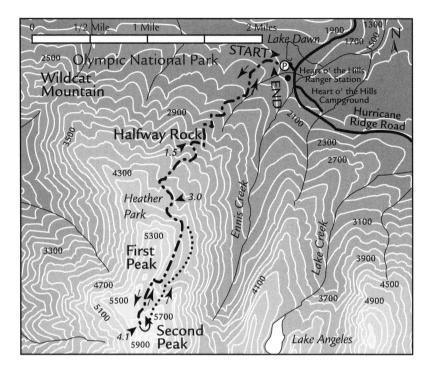

Here's an alpine, north-facing bowl that is seldom visited in winter because you've got to carry your gear up a steep, no-nonsense trail for at least 2 miles to snow. Take considerable consolation as you huff and puff up in knowing that the powder and stunning view will very likely belong to you, and you alone.

Your trail begins at the south end of the parking lot. Don't mistake it for the Lake Angeles Trail, which starts on the east side of the lot. The gentle first quarter mile of the trail is also likely to deceive, because of the climb ahead.

The climb is straightforward, switching back along a heavily forested ridge above a tributary to Ennis Creek. It climbs in switchback after switchback to the south-southwest, passing Halfway Rock only about one-third of the way to Second Peak.

Continue climbing to about 3,500 feet, where you'll probably be able to don skis or snowshoes and climb into Heather Park at about 4,000 feet past a big rock guarding the open slopes above. These slopes are your playland, underneath First Peak, directly to the south, and Second Peak, around the shoulder of First Peak to the east.

For the best view both north and south, climb to the flat saddle between First and Second Peaks by turning east at about the 4,500-foot level in

Heather Park. Climb around a north-facing ridge and traverse up its east face to the saddle to the south.

Second Peak is 500 feet higher, due south. If there's time, enjoy the view before swooping back through Heather Park. Look north to Port Angeles, Ediz Hook, the Strait of Juan de Fuca, and Vancouver Island. Look south to all those Olympic Mountains, hiding all that untracked, wild snow.

66 THE OLYMPICS
Deer Park
❄❄❄½

Distance:	6.0 to 14.0 miles
Base elevation:	3,400 feet
Elevation gain:	2,600 feet
Trail time:	4 to 8 hours
Trail type:	Gravel road
Skill level:	Intermediate
Avalanche potential:	Moderate
Traction advisory:	Skins, waxable
Maps:	Green Trails 135; Custom Correct, Elwha Valley; USGS Maiden Peak, Tyler Peak (7.5' series)

A mountain goat in winter garb visits the summit of Blue Mountain.

Getting There

From Seattle, first head toward the Hood Canal Bridge via one of two routes. Either take the ferry to Winslow on Bainbridge Island and drive up State Route 305 about 21 miles; or drive north on I-5 to Edmonds, and from there take the ferry to Kingston and drive west on SR 104 about 13 miles to the bridge. It's a little over an hour either way, but ferry lines can make the trip longer. From the bridge, drive west on SR 104 to US Highway 101 at Discovery Bay. Follow US 101 north and west through Sequim toward Port Angeles. Just before entering Port Angeles, at the cinema complex on the left, turn left up Deer Park Road. Follow the road about 9 miles to the Olympic National Park boundary. If the road is gated at this point, take your snowriding to Hurricane Ridge or be prepared for a long slog up a gravel road. If the gate is open, continue up the road until snow or another gate at about 3,500 feet elevation stops you. It is 8 miles, one way, from the park boundary to Deer Park. During most winters, you'll be skiing or shoeing about 4.5 miles of that.

The Route

0.0   Deer Park Road
4.5   Deer Park
5.2   Blue Mountain summit

A half century ago, before the Hurricane Ridge Road was built, Olympic Peninsula skiers piled into their cars and slipped and slid up the steep, narrow Deer Park Road to Blue Mountain, where you could ride one of those newfangled rope tows up the mountain.

Today, the rope tow has been moved to Hurricane Ridge and the only way to get to Deer Park is by the power of your lungs and legs. This road ski through alpine forest to wide-open slopes and the summit of Blue Mountain might be a good choice for downhillers in the spring. But it makes a good tour for cross-country adventurers seeking solitude in midwinter.

The best way to figure how far you've got to go on foot after encountering snow or a locked gate is by noting your car's odometer reading as you pass the park boundary, 9 miles from US Highway 101, with 8 miles still to go to Deer Park.

The road ascends through forest and provides good midwinter snow, but can be icy during the spring. Climb on the road around several switchbacks until gaining the ridge leading beneath Blue Mountain to Deer Park. Greatest

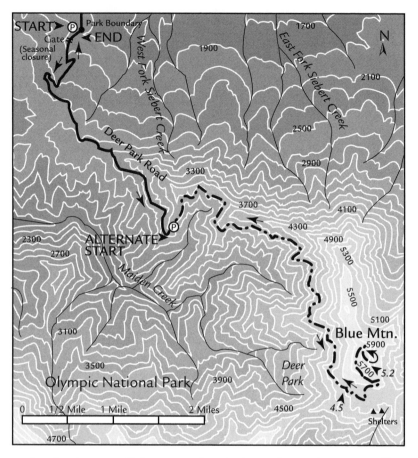

avalanche danger will be encountered where the road crosses gullies sweeping down from Blue Mountain.

Deer Park is a broad, south-facing alpine saddle that holds a summer campground and mind-melting views of the Olympic Mountains. You'll find a summer ranger station there, an old barn, and two three-sided backcountry shelters that make good weekend destinations.

Once at Deer Park, climb Blue Mountain to the north, switching back at about 5,500 feet along the western slope. You'll find an incredible east-facing bowl with about 800 vertical feet of open slopes. This slope may be corniced, so don't jump off until you've made certain your will is in order.

The ridge to the southwest is also a good springtime hill in some conditions, but is frequently windblown or scoured to bare ground. On sunny spring days, the slope is redolent of sprouting wild onion.

67
THE OLYMPICS
High Divide
❄❄❄½

Distance: 17.0 miles
Base elevation: 1,900 feet
Elevation gain: 3,200 feet
Trail time: 9 hours
Trail type: Summer trail
Skill level: Intermediate
Avalanche potential: Moderate
Traction advisory: Skins, waxable
Maps: Green Trails 133, 134; Custom Correct, Seven Lakes Basin-Hoh; USGS Bogachiel Peak, Mount Carrie (7.5' series)

Clouds hover above the Hoh Valley at High Divide.

Getting There

From Seattle, first head toward the Hood Canal Bridge via one of two routes. Either take the ferry to Winslow on Bainbridge Island and drive up State Route 305 about 21 miles; or drive north on I-5 to Edmonds, and from there take the ferry to Kingston and drive west on SR 104 about 13 miles to the bridge. It's a little over an hour either way, but ferry lines can make the trip longer. From the bridge, drive west on SR 104 to US Highway 101 at Discovery Bay. Follow US 101 north and west through Sequim to Port Angeles. Turn left on Race Street to bypass the downtown area. Follow Race Street to Lauridsen Boulevard and turn right. Lauridsen leads west back to US 101 and the western outskirts of the city.

Turn left on US 101 and follow it 30 miles west, past Lake Crescent, to the Sol Duc Hot Springs Road.

Turn left on the Sol Duc Hot Springs Road. Though paved and usually snow free throughout the winter, it may be closed at the fee booth at the entrance to Olympic National Park. If so, plan your snowriding adventure elsewhere, because it is 14 miles up the road to the Sol Duc River trailhead. But if the road is open, drive to the trailhead, 1.7 miles south of Sol Duc Hot Springs Resort.

The Route

- **0.0** Sol Duc River trailhead
- **0.9** Sol Duc Falls; trail forks, turn left
- **4.9** Appleton Pass Trail junction; keep right
- **5.6** Upper Sol Duc Camp; climb left
- **5.8** Foot log
- **6.5** Lower Sol Duc Park; foot log
- **7.0** Foot log or snow bridge
- **7.1** Upper Sol Duc Park
- **8.0** Heart Lake
- **8.5** High Divide

Encumbered only by skis and a light day pack (containing, of course, all the food and gear to survive a winter night in an emergency bivouac), strong snowriders can climb to High Divide and get a pleasurable 1,000-vertical-foot run in a broad alpine bowl before dodging trees. In most winters, snow is ski-able down to the Upper Sol Duc Camp.

If you have a weekend, backpack to Upper Sol Duc Camp and ski or ride on the divide in the afternoon and next morning. Boarders with snowshoes

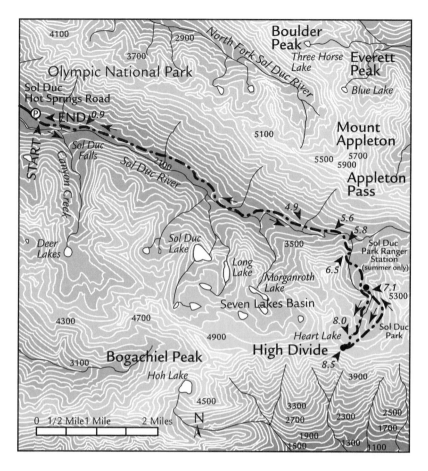

may find this route more accessible because the hike to snow is long and the snow usually begins rather abruptly between 3,000 and 4,000 feet.

Begin by walking the flat trail to Sol Duc Falls, where you'll find a shelter and a fork in the trail. The way to the left leads to High Divide; the right fork crosses the river and climbs to Deer Lake.

Take the left fork, climb above the shelter, and follow the trail for a couple of miles through a nice open meadow where elk can often be seen in the winter. The trail continues upstream on the northern bank of the river, eventually switching back to climb away from the river on a flat bench where, at 4.9 miles, it forks. Take the right fork, which leads to High Divide. The left fork climbs to Appleton Pass.

The trail enters a second meadow, which may be snow-covered, before climbing through the forest to Upper Sol Duc Camp at 5.6 miles. A shelter once located here was wiped out by a massive avalanche in the 1970s.

Turn left above the river and climb another fifth of a mile to a foot-log crossing of the Sol Duc. This high log may have up to a foot of snow on it, but has a sturdy rail for balance.

The trail is usually still easily followed as it climbs southeast above the river, now on the left. It switches back twice, but when snow cover is adequate, you can climb the broad timbered ridge above the cascading Sol Duc. At about 4,000 feet, the trail crosses a snow-covered bench and begins a traverse through timber down into the Sol Duc canyon, where a foot log crosses the river at Lower Sol Duc Park at 6.5 miles.

If snow is too deep here to cross the log, follow the river into Lower Sol Duc Park, keeping as close to the river on flats as possible to avoid an obvious avalanche slope on the right. You'll find a snow bridge at the head of the meadows. Cross here and find the trail as it skirts a wide meadow to the southeast and climbs into woods.

The route steepens here, climbing a ridge above the tumbling river and crossing one fork at 7.0 miles on a foot log. As likely as not, this crossing will be on a snow bridge in the winter. Climb the ridge to an open meadow at 7.1 miles, Upper Sol Duc Park.

Two routes are possible from here. For the first, the trail recrosses the river and climbs through a clearing visible across the river to the west. For the second route, continue through trees at the west end of the meadow and climb into the alpine bowl to the west. Though more direct, this way passes under avalanche slopes.

In either case, aim for the low point in the ridge to the west, which is the south end of the High Divide. Before you get there, you'll enter a second basin just below the divide that contains Heart Lake.

For the best view and downhill ride, climb west along the crest of the divide for about half a mile to a broad meadow. You can drop to the southeast to Heart Lake from here, getting a downhill run all the way to Lower Sol Duc Park.

But as long as you got this far, you might as well stare across the green valley of the Hoh River to the Blue Glacier on Mount Olympus, which, if you are an Olympic raven, is only 5 miles away.

68 THE OLYMPICS
Potholes
❄❄❄

Distance:	10.2 miles
Base elevation:	1,900 feet
Elevation gain:	3,800 feet
Trail time:	6 hours
Trail type:	Summer trail
Skill level:	Intermediate
Avalanche potential:	Moderate
Traction advisory:	Skins, waxable
Maps:	Green Trails 133; Custom Correct, Seven Lakes Basin-Hoh; USGS Bogachiel Peak (7.5' series)

Getting There

From Seattle, first head toward the Hood Canal Bridge via one of two routes. Either take the ferry to Winslow on Bainbridge Island and drive up State Route 305 about 21 miles; or drive north on I-5 to Edmonds, and from there take the ferry to Kingston and drive west on SR 104 about 13 miles to the bridge. It's a little over an hour either way, but ferry lines can make the trip longer. From the bridge, drive west on SR 104 to US Highway 101 at Discovery Bay. Follow US 101 north and west through Sequim to Port Angeles. Turn left on Race Street to bypass the downtown area. Follow Race Street to Lauridsen Boulevard and turn right. Lauridsen leads west back to US 101 and the western outskirts of the city.

Turn left on US 101 and follow it 30 miles west, past Lake Crescent, to the Sol Duc Hot Springs Road.

Turn left on the Sol Duc Hot Springs Road. Though paved and usually snow free throughout the winter, it may be closed at the fee booth at the entrance to Olympic National Park. If so, plan your snowriding adventure elsewhere, because it is 14 miles up the road to the Sol Duc River trailhead. But if the road is open, drive to the trailhead, 1.7 miles south of Sol Duc Hot Springs Resort.

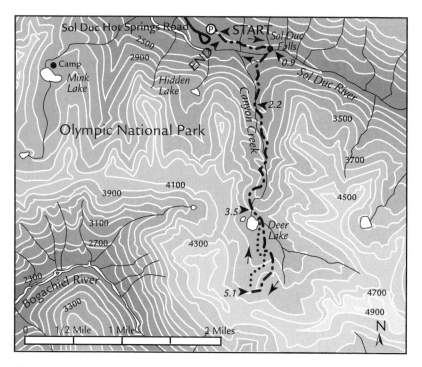

The Route

0.0 Sol Duc River trailhead
0.9 Sol Duc Falls; trail forks, turn right
1.1 Trail forks, keep left
2.2 Canyon Creek
3.5 Deer Lake
4.0 Trail forks, keep left
5.1 Potholes meadows

Here's another trail you'll likely begin in telemark or boarding boots, carrying your downhill gear and day pack. The run through wide-spaced evergreen trunks down to Deer Lake is usually in sheltered, softly settled powder, and parts of the trail below can provide plenty of challenge or opportunities for a fir sandwich.

Begin by following the flat trail to Sol Duc Falls, where the trail forks at the shelter. Take the right fork down and across a pony bridge above Sol Duc Falls.

Climb up the trail, passing to the left at the Lover's Lane Trail fork at 1.1 miles. The trail climbs above Canyon Creek to a log bridge across the creek at

2.2 miles and, after the bridge, switches back to climb above the west side of the creek through an obvious avalanche path from the west.

The trail continues to climb above Canyon Creek, which lives up to its name the higher you climb. Stay out of the canyon on the west side if you lose the trail as it switches back several times, indicated by orange markers on tree trunks.You'll probably encounter steady snow between 3,000 feet and Deer Lake at 3.5 miles and 3,500 feet.

The trail crosses Canyon Creek on a log bridge as it empties out of Deer Lake. Follow the trail around the left, or east, shore of the lake to the south end, where the trail forks. Keep left here, climbing the ridge above a long, open meadow holding one of the creeks that drains into Deer Lake.

The trail rounds this creek basin on benches and at the south end switches back to the flat alpine meadow that holds the Potholes, a number of alpine tarns in a basin below the 4,500-foot-high ridge that divides the Sol Duc and Bogachiel River drainages.

If time permits, climb to the lowest point in the ridge to the south for the best downhill run and a good view of the Bogachiel River basin. From this saddle, you can ride directly north into the Potholes meadows, then down through forest to the Deer Lake basin.

69 | THE OLYMPICS
Mount Ellinor

❄❄❄❄

Distance:	4.0 to 8.0 miles
Base elevation:	3,500 feet
Elevation gain:	2,500 feet
Trail time:	4 to 7 hours
Trail type:	Forest road, summer trail, backcountry
Skill level:	Advanced
Avalanche potential:	Moderate
Traction advisory:	Skins, waxable
Maps:	Green Trails 167; Custom Correct, Mount Skokomish-Lake Cushman; USGS Mount Washington (7.5' series)

Getting There

From Seattle, drive south on I-5 to Tacoma. From there, head north across the Narrows Bridge on State Route 16 for about 20 miles to Gorst and SR 3. Follow SR 3 south through Belfair to SR 106. Drive around the south shore of Hood Canal on SR 106 to Potlatch and US Highway 101.

Take US 101 north to Hoodsport. Turn left on the Lake Cushman Road and follow it past Lake Cushman State Park to a T intersection with Forest Road 245. Turn right on FR 245 and drive for 1.7 miles to FR 2419.

Forest Road 2419 climbs steeply into the Big Creek valley below Mount Ellinor and Mount Washington. During most winters, you can drive to around 2,500 to 3,000 feet, leaving you about 2 to 3 miles of road skiing before you reach the junction with FR 014, the official start for this route.

The Route

0.0 Forest Road 2419 junction with Forest Road 014
1.0 Forest Road 014 ends; climb right
2.0 Ellinor chute
3.0 Ellinor summit

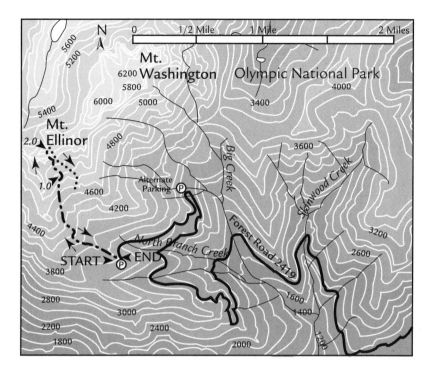

This is another straightforward, no-nonsense climb that might be better suited to snowboard-toting snowshoers than cross-country skiers. The lower part of the road can be a good ski tour for families when conditions permit.

From snow line, climb on Forest Road 2419 up the Big Creek valley, crossing to the west side of the valley at about 2,800 feet. Stay on the road past the Lower Ellinor trailhead, following the road for about a mile to the switchback junction with FR 014.

Turn left on FR 014 and climb it about a mile to its end. Take Upper Ellinor trailhead, on the right, which climbs the hogback ridge to a junction with Mount Ellinor Trail 812 at about 3,300 feet. Trail 812 then switches back through the forest for about 400 feet before traversing north to a bench and climbing into meadows at about 4,600 feet. A chute begins at the north end of these meadows and climbs steeply 1,000 feet to a basin just below 5,994-foot Mount Ellinor.

The meadows below the chute are a good turnaround point in the winter when weather is bad or avalanche hazard is high. When conditions allow, climb the chute. It is shaped like an hourglass, curving to the east slightly at its narrowest point.

In spring or ideal winter conditions, the chute offers a good ride down for advanced telemark skiers and boarders accustomed to slopes of 30 degrees or more. An ice ax or self-arrest grips on ski poles can be a comfort when climbing the chute on morning hardpack. And remember that snow conditions can change dramatically in the 1,000 vertical feet from the bottom to the top of the chute.

From the 5,700-foot-high basin at the top of the chute, turn northwest and climb the slopes just south of the summit, making the final climb to the north. Follow your tracks back down after ogling the view, which includes Lake Cushman far below, Mount Washington next door, Mount Rainier to the southeast, and hundreds of Olympic peaks to the north.

70

Olympic Hot Springs

❄

Distance:	7.6 miles
Base elevation:	1,700 feet
Elevation gain:	350 feet
Trail time:	4 hours
Trail type:	Paved road
Skill level:	Novice
Avalanche potential:	Low
Traction advisory:	Waxable, waxless
Maps:	Green Trails 134; Custom Correct, Elwha Valley; USGS Mount Carrie (7.5' series)

Getting There

From Seattle, first head toward the Hood Canal Bridge via one of two routes. Either take the ferry to Winslow on Bainbridge Island and drive up State Route 305 about 21 miles; or drive north on I-5 to Edmonds, and from there take the ferry to Kingston and drive west on SR 104 about 13 miles to the bridge. It's a little over an hour either way, but ferry lines can make the trip longer. From the bridge, drive west on SR 104 to US Highway 101 at Discovery Bay. Follow US 101 north and west through Sequim to Port Angeles. Turn left on Race Street to bypass the downtown area. Follow Race Street to Lauridsen Boulevard and turn right. Lauridsen leads west back to US 101 and the western outskirts of the city.

Turn left on US 101 and follow it 9 miles to the Elwha River Road. Turn left on the Elwha River Road, noting its intersection with the Little River Road after about a tenth of a mile, and follow Elwha River Road past the Olympic National Park entrance station. If the station is open, you'll be asked to pay a $10 per carload entrance fee. (If the fee booth is closed, as it may be in the winter, simply continue on your way.)

Stay on the Elwha River Road past its junction with Whiskey Bend Road. From the junction, cross the Elwha River and drive another 3.8 miles on Boulder Creek Road to a gate at the Lake Mills overlook. The gate will likely

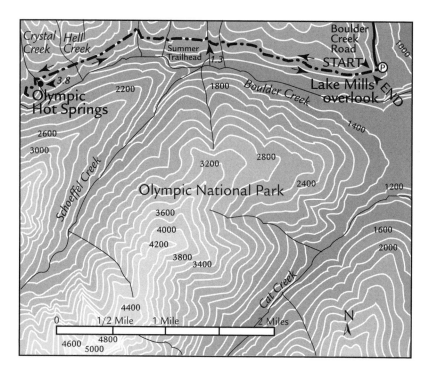

be closed in winter. In summer, the road is open for another 1.3 miles up the Boulder Creek valley.

The Route

0.0   Lake Mills overlook parking area

1.3   Olympic Hot Springs trailhead

3.8   Olympic Hot Springs

Even if all you do is carry your skis or board to Olympic Hot Springs and float them in a pool beside you—even if you have to hike or ride your mountain bike into these wild hot springs after eating Hurricane Ridge powder all day—you owe yourself a winter soak.

Because of its low elevation, the country around Olympic Hot Springs is usually not snow-covered. But because the road is not maintained beyond Lake Mills, whatever snow falls in the winter accumulates until the spring thaw. When adequate snow covers the road, this makes a good cross-country tour for the entire family.

The road climbs gently and steadily for the entire distance to the hot springs, dropping twice to cross streams along the way before climbing to the old parking area at the springs. For a soak, follow the trail at the west end of the parking area for about a quarter mile to a bridge across Boulder Creek, turn right, and pick any one of several pools uphill or downhill from the trail. (Caution! You may encounter naked people, with bodies very similar to yours, soaking in the pools. If nudity offends you, flee rapidly or close your eyes.)

Going Farther

While the backcountry slopes of the Cascades are the most convenient to many telemarkers and snowboarders, they by no means offer the most consistent and best snow or weather. To find that, you've got to go east, young person.

Yes, even farther east than the dry snow of the Okanogan. The best snow in the state—and some excellent slopes on 7,000-foot-high cloud gougers—will be found in the Kettle Range north and south of 5,575-foot Sherman Pass.

Follow US Highway 395 and State Route 20 northwest of Spokane for about 100 miles, and you're at the Sherman Pass Sno-Park. Park on the north side of the highway and ski south to 7,103-foot Snow Peak or north to 7,135-foot Copper Butte. If you'd like more information about the area, contact the Kettle Falls Ranger Station, (509) 738-6111.

Another faraway spot is the hill around the Deer Creek Summit Sno-Park, northeast of the town of Curlew, about 12 miles north of Republic on the British Columbia border. For information about the area, call the Republic Ranger Station, (509) 775-3305.

Most remote of all are the mountains of the Salmo-Priest Wilderness in the extreme northeastern corner of the state. Here are 7,300-foot mountains like Gypsy Peak, where logging roads provide access by snowmobile or long cross-country ski tours from Sullivan Lake. For information, contact the Sullivan Lake Ranger District, (509) 446-7580.

The fortunate snowriders of Eastern Washington can find wild, dry white stuff only 30 minutes from downtown Spokane on 5,200-foot Mount Spokane. Though served by lifts on the east slope, the mountain has a huge west-facing meadow where it isn't difficult to find untracked powder. For information, call the Mount Spokane State Park recording, (509) 238-4025.

Finally, you'll find some accessible wild snow around the beautiful Blue Mountains of southeastern Washington. Explore the country around the Boundary Sno-Park, or visit the area around Ski Bluewood, southeast of Dayton. For information, call the Pomeroy Ranger Station, (509) 843-1891.

Closer to home for most of us is the excellent groomed or track cross-country skiing in the Cascades. Scottish Lakes High Camp offers more than 17 miles of backcountry trails in the Chiwaukum Mountains on the edge of the Alpine Lakes Wilderness. You'll find great road skiing through mature forest, clear-cut slopes for telemarking or riding, and day trips to high alpine adventures above timberline. Guests at Scottish Lake ride to the high camp aboard a sno-cat or snowmobiles, or can ski in or out to private cabins furnished with propane stove and lanterns, woodstove, and cookware. You bring your food and sleeping bag. For information, call High Country Adventures, (888) 944-2267.

More fine backcountry snowriding can be found along the white ways of the Mount Tahoma Trails Association, a nonprofit volunteer group that tends more than 100 miles of groomed and ungroomed trails and hills along in the western foothills of Mount Rainier. The association maintains three huts and a yurt in the backcountry, and hut-to-hut skiing is popular with members who pay $15 per year—although use of the trails is free to anyone with a state Sno-Park permit. Overnight stays at the huts are also free to members who pay a refundable reservation deposit and minimal processing fee. Huts are equipped, at a minimum, with heaters, lanterns, tables, and sleeping lofts. For information about the association, write Mount Tahoma Trails Association, PO Box 206, Ashford, WA 98304; or call the association's office in season, (360) 569-2451.

Several winter resort areas offer groomed cross-country trails that provide access to wild snow. Expect to pay trail fees at these areas, generally under $10 per day.

Perhaps the most extensive trail system is the Nordic Center at The Summit at Snoqualmie. Here you'll find more than 30 miles of machine-groomed trails for kicking and gliding or skating, including lift-served access to Mount Catherine and Silver Peak, Routes 38 and 39 in this book. Besides these hills, snowriders testing the upper trails will find a number of clear-cut slopes offering as much as 500 vertical feet of ungroomed white stuff. For information about the area, call (425) 434-6646, or the ski-conditions hotline in season, (206) 236-1600.

The Stevens Pass Nordic Center provides more than 15 miles of groomed trails for striders and skaters. The center, just east of Stevens Pass on US Highway 2, manages trails that lead past a number of clear-cut slopes offering good downhill opportunities on ungroomed snow. For information about the Stevens Pass Nordic Center, call (360) 973-2441 in season.

In the Okanogan, the Methow Valley Ski Touring Association offers the most extensive groomed cross-country trail system in the western United States, with more than 120 miles of striding and skating. You'll find everything from hut-to-hut skiing to helicopter access to the backcountry. Although trails around the Methow generally appeal to cross-country skiers who enjoy touring over rolling hills, some of the white routes provide access to challenging, open slopes. You also might meet some of the local skiers who are in no small measure responsible for the popularity of backcountry snowriding, folks like Don Portman and Steve Barnett. For information about the Methow Valley Ski Touring Association, call (509) 996-3287.

The Loup Loup Ski Bowl, just across Highway 20 from Loup Loup, Route 50 in this book, provides a 20-mile web of groomed trails with opportunities along some for downhill skiing or boarding in wild snow. For information on cross-country skiing at Loup Loup, call (509) 923-2142.

Two other winter resorts—White Pass and Mount Baker—offer groomed trails for cross-country skiers. The White Pass trail system provides access to the first leg of the Sand Lake tour, Route 24 in this book, while the short Baker trail leads to the beginning of the Herman Saddle trip, Route 55 in this book. For information about White Pass cross-country skiing, call (509) 672-3106 in season; for Baker, call (206) 634-0200 in season.

Extending the Season

As of April 1998, my good friend Jim Drannan, a.k.a. the Gnarly Dude, has carved up at least 1,000 vertical feet of Washington State snow every month for 101 consecutive months. If there is any doubt that you can get a good ride on wild snow any time of the year in this state, a conversation with the Dude will set it aside immediately.

Most skiers and boarders who want to ride long after the snow has stopped falling look to the state's big snow cones: Mounts Baker, Rainier, St. Helens, and Adams. Each provides excellent spring skiing well into summer, and one or two can give you splendid downhill through the fall until the snow flies.

If you are among those who just can't wait until next season, visit the south slopes of Mount Baker. Ptarmigan Ridge, Route 54 in this book, provides good slopes at least until mid-June. The Sholes Glacier above shines white until blue ice shows through in the fall.

As it does in the winter, Mount Rainier yields marvelous snowfields almost through autumn. You can ride the upper Muir Snowfield, Route 11 in this book, until the sun cups of August look like the Grand Canyon.

Then it's time to move to the north side of Tahoma, where you'll find more vertical than you can handle in a single day on the remnant Russell and Flett Glaciers and even parts of the massive Carbon Glacier. On the right days and with the right equipment and training, you can ride off the top of Rainier on the Emmons Glacier most any summer day.

The descent of Mount Rainier via the Emmons route—or any route from the summit—involves skills and knowledge beyond the scope of this book. Generally speaking, if you want to ski or board above 9,000 feet on the north side of the mountain or 10,000 feet from Camp Muir, you must first learn and practice such mountaineering skills as ice ax arrest, roped travel, crevasse rescue, and self-rescue.

Those less inclined to tackle technical climbing can explore the Frying Pan Glacier above Panhandle Gap, or find more than 2,000 vertical feet of downhill on Inter Glacier in July. Inter Glacier is usually crevasse-free well into July. When the Sunrise area opens around July, there's big air and big snow to be found off the three Burroughs peaks.

Farther south, Mount St. Helens opens its southern slopes around May and the wild snow there usually provides good riding for at least a month before the sun starts digging huge wells in it. If you plan to ski St. Helens in July, you'll need 240-centimeter jumping skis just to span the sun cups.

Mount Adams can give you about 3,000 vertical feet of snowriding from the summit down to Lunch Counter on the eastern ridge of the 12,000-footer. In July, you'll probably only have to carry skis or board about 3 miles before hitting snow, and the snowfield above 9,000-foot Lunch Counter is usually navigable on skis through mid-August.

In the fall and late spring, snowriders can get closer to such places as Cutthroat Pass, Route 53 in this book, by driving east from Newhalem on the North Cascades Highway, State Route 20. You'll find a number of hills, including an awesomely steep couloir at Washington Pass.

Another good spring tour to good hills is Chinook Pass and Tipsoo Peak off State Route 410. Ideal time to hit Chinook Pass is when State Route 123, Cayuse Pass, is open but Chinook Pass remains closed. This time varies, but a good time to check is the last two weeks in April.

At last, we have reached the end of this trail, the time to peel our climbing skins from our skis and look back on this silent, splendid winter world below. Gaze with me from this summit, across the mountains we have climbed with our eyes and with our minds, and consider this final fact: If you begin your snowriding in December and whip down at least one of the hills outlined in this book every Saturday and Sunday through February, you won't have to look for a new place to ride for three years. Bon appétit!

Resources

Following are some important telephone numbers and Web sites for back-country skiers and boarders:

Snow and weather conditions

Cascade Ski Report	(206) 634-0200
Northwest Avalanche Center Hotline	(206) 526-6677
U.S. Weather Service	(206) 526-6087

or check the following Web site, which is full of info for snowriders and other outdoorsfolk: www.gorp.com/wow

Washington Dept. of Transportation mountain pass highway report (in winter)   (888) 766-4636

or check the following Web site: www.wsdot.wa.gov/Traveler/ TravelInfo.htm

Backcountry winter recreation clubs

The Mountaineers	(206) 284-6310
Washington Alpine Club hotline	(206) 467-2619
Washington Ski Touring Club information	(206) 525-4451

Backcountry information for routes in this book

Cle Elum Ranger Station (Blewett Pass, Salmon La Sac)	(509) 674-4411
Glacier Public Service Center (Mount Baker)	(360) 599-2714
Leavenworth Ranger Station (Blewett Pass)	(509) 782-1413
Mount Rainier National Park recording	(360) 569-2211
Mount St. Helens information	(360) 247-3903
Mount St. Helens climbing information	(360) 247-3961
Naches Ranger Station (White Pass)	(509) 653-2205
Nisqually Entrance (Mount Rainier)	(360) 569-2211, ext. 2390
North Bend Ranger Station (Snoqualmie)	(425) 888-1421
Olympic National Park recording	(360) 452-0329
Olympic Wilderness Information Center	(360) 452-0300
Packwood Ranger Station (White Pass)	(360) 494-0600
Paradise Ranger Station (Mount Rainier)	(360) 569-2211, ext. 2314
Sedro Woolley Ranger Station (Mount Baker)	(360) 856-5700
Skykomish Ranger Station (Stevens Pass)	(360) 677-2414

Trout Lake Ranger Station (Mount Adams)	(509) 395-2501
Twisp Ranger Station (Okanogan)	(509) 997-2131
Wenatchee National Forest (Mission Ridge)	(509) 662-4335
White River Ranger Station (Crystal Mountain)	(360) 825-6585
Winthrop Ranger Station (Okanogan)	(509) 996-2266

Recommended Reading

Daffern, Tony. *Avalanche Safety for Skiers and Climbers*. Calgary, Alberta, Canada: Rocky Mountain Books, 1983.

Fredston, Jill A., and Douglas S. Fesler. *Snow Sense: A Guide to Evaluating Snow Avalanche Hazard*. Anchorage, Alaska: Alaska Mountain Safety Center, Inc., 1994.

McClung, David, and Peter Schaerer. *The Avalanche Handbook*. Seattle, Washington: The Mountaineers, 1993.

O'Bannon, Allen. *Allen and Mike's Really Cool Backcountry Ski Book*. Evergreen, Colorado: Chockstone Press, 1996.

Parker, Paul. *Free Heel Skiing*. Seattle, Washington: The Mountaineers, 1995.

Townsend, Chris. *Wilderness Skiing and Winter Camping*. Camden, Maine: Ragged Mountain Press, 1994.